OPSHOPULENCE

PRAISE FOR *OPSHOPULENCE*

'Faye is a sartorial alchemist. She has a magic ability to create what others can't, mixing fossicked treasures with equal parts vision and love.

Through fashion, Faye builds aspiration and a sense of community. She sees the beauty in discarded items and gives them and their wearers a "Cinderella" moment: inspired by Chanel, Gucci, and Gaultier.

Most of all, Faye has the kind of energy you just want to be around. Warm, inspiring, generous, and infectiously up-beat. Faye's wisdom, styling knowledge and optimism are exactly what the world needs right now. Your wardrobe, eco-footprint and wallet will thank you.'

Katrina Blowers, Television Newsreader, Award-Winning Journalist, Podcaster and Author

'Over the past few years, I've had the pleasure of creating magical TV moments with thrifty, eco-stylist, Faye De Lanty. Her ability to turn discarded, unwanted items into must-have, high-fashion looks is truly inspiring to watch.

More importantly, Faye cares about each and every woman she styles. She takes the time to understand who they are as individuals in a warm and engaging way before delving deep into their archives to demonstrate how they can re-invent their wardrobes and re-invigorate their love of fashion.

Faye is the Queen of transformations, helping women look and feel fabulous, with a clean conscience and without spending a fortune—bonus! Her creative and innovative ideas using belts, scarves and brooches shows us how easy and achievable it is to turn one look into hundreds.

Faye's likeability is the cherry on top, making her exceptional TV talent and a pleasure to work with.

This is the book we all need to embrace second hand fashion, elevate our wardrobes, and discover our own unique sense of style.'

Britt Cohen, Reporter, Today Show, Australia

'Faye is positive, creative, and passionate. She is always developing new ideas on ways we can not only engage our current community but grow this by making shopping second hand accessible to all. We are proud to have Faye work with us at Salvos Stores.'

Salvos Stores Executive Leadership Team

'Faye is a true professional and creative mastermind. She's at the forefront of the fashion industry and a leader in sustainable, eco and recycled clothing.

Her creativity is second to none. What she brings to life for our television segments always inspires and excites. Faye is a self-starter and essentially produces herself which is rare to come across.

We can always rely on Faye to deliver… and with that… she always brings a smile, calmness and a beautiful demeanour that is infectious to be around.'

Sarah Mason, Senior Producer, Entertainment STUDIO 10

'In bounced this spritely 17-year-old pocket rocket with an infectious smile and an enthusiasm for life that was a perfect fit for Totally Wild. Having now known "DeLant" for more than a quarter century, I can attest to the fact that she is one special human. Fashionista aside, she is always kind, always generous, always loads of fun—just great to be around.

Our incredibly creative fashion focused DeLant, was already designing her own eco pieces at just 18, rocking on in with style and confidence, wearing her unique tie-dye singlets with beautifully applied and hand stitched cotton doily flowers with vintage blue jeans.

Sustainably mindful and environmentally aware, her passion is evident in everything she does. A continuous contributor to her eco styling craft, Faye has changed the way to look at and wear clothing.

To say I'm privileged to know her and am incredibly proud of what she's achieved, is an absolute understatement. There will only ever be one De Lant and I love her so.'

Kim Bramble, Senior Marketing, Event and Production Manager

Published in Australia by
Evolve Publishing
PO BOX 221 246 Oxford St Paddington NSW 2021
faye@fashionhound.tv
www.fashionhound.tv
www.opshopulence.com

First published in Australia 2022
Copyright © Faye De Lanty 2022

All rights reserved. No part of this publication may be reproduced, stored in a retrieval system, or transmitted, in any form or by any means without the prior written permission of the publisher, nor be otherwise circulated in any form of binding or cover other than that in which it is published and without a similar condition being imposed on the subsequent purchaser.

National Library of Australia Cataloguing in Publication entry

 A catalogue record for this book is available from the National Library of Australia

ISBN: 978-0-6450710-0-9 (paperback)
ISBN: 978-0-6450710-1-6 (hardback)
ISBN: 978-0-6450710-3-0 (epub)

Cover design by Lillia Gerasimchuk
Book layout design by Sophie White

Printed by Ingram Spark

Disclaimer: All care has been taken in the preparation of the information herein, but no responsibility can be accepted by the publisher or author for any damages resulting from the misinterpretation of this work. All contact details given in this book were current at the time of publication, but are subject to change.

The advice given in this book is based on the experience of the individuals. Professionals should be consulted for individual problems. The author and publisher shall not be responsible for any person with regard to any loss or damage caused directly or indirectly by the information in this book.

Opshopulence

How to make thrift store
look like couture

...and save the planet

Faye De Lanty

*To my mum Nadia and my dad Mick,
who designed me with equal parts of their Opshopulent selves,
thrifty creativity, an eye for finery, and the hustle incarnate.*

*The ultimate cheerleader—my divine husband Lee—
for loving me unconditionally and believing
in my Opshopulence even before I did.*

Lastly but certainly not least, my beloved dog-angel above—Soho.

*Soho taught me to follow my nose and never give up
on the insatiable desire for a tasty treat,
in my case that has and always will be the story of style.*

My never-ending fashion fairytale.

CONTENTS

About The Author		10
Contributors		11
Foreword		13
Introduction	You Are What You Wear	15
Chapter 1	Why We Need a Fashion Revolution	31
Chapter 2	Enclothed Cognition	71
Chapter 3	From Restriction to Reinvention	87
Chapter 4	The ABC of Opshopulence	105
Chapter 5	Developing Your Signature Opshopulent Style	115
Chapter 6	Op Shop Decoder	129
Chapter 7	30 Things to Thrift	141
Chapter 8	Let Reuse Be Your Muse	161
Chapter 9	The Wardrobe Workout	211
Chapter 10	The Charity Shop Challenge	229
Chapter 11	The Opshopulent Man	237
Chapter 12	Next Gen Opshopulence	251
Chapter 13	Opshopulence Interview Series	263
Conclusion		315
Endnotes		326
Bibliography		327
Glossary of Terms—A Thrift-Saurus		329
Colloquial/Faye-isms		332
Acknowledgments		333
Author Contact		335

ABOUT THE AUTHOR

Faye De Lanty is a pre-loved chic pioneer. As eco-stylist for The Salvation Army in Australia, it's Faye's job to educate, empower and inspire consumers to think sustainably and act mindfully with their fashion and lifestyle choices.

Faye works tirelessly to shift perceptions and transform how we see second hand. From visual merchandising, social media strategy, eco-events, and branding concepts to presenting regular fashion segments on national morning TV.

Faye is all about reusing, recycling, and reducing our textile waste without ever sacrificing style.

With a background in environmental kid's television, Faye was the co-host of Network Ten's highly successful children's program *Totally Wild* for a decade.

Faye's Instagram community is a highly engaged eco-hub for shared learning, creative self-expression and inspiring sustainable style.

Her blog, Fashion Hound, is the go-to for tips, tricks, and thrifty hacks.

Faye is based in Sydney, Australia, with the love of her life, husband Lee. Together they go on thrift adventures and enjoy nothing more than to shape-shift an occasion with extreme Opshopulence!

Instagram @fayedelanty
Website www.fashionhound.tv

CONTRIBUTORS

@powersheis

Studio Images

Vivienne is a strategic creative, whose business foundations are based on her core values of female empowerment, equality, diversity and creative expression. From shooting with high-profile individuals, to brands, fashion and women of all types. Viv has created a community who look to step outside the social constructs of standardized beauty, educating on the importance of beauty coming from within, and stepping into their light.

Illustrations

Sydney-based next-generation sustainable-fashion activist, stylist and illustrator. Indi Field has been in the sustainable fashion game for over three years, educating her generation on the benefits of thrift and upcycling our style.

Indi has been an artist since she was young, and just recently emerged into illustrations and fashion art.

Between school, her local job, and volunteering as a lifeguard, she has managed to grow a following on Instagram **@thriftwithindi**, where she shares OODTs, fashion tips, and 'thrift flips.'

@thriftwithindi

FOREWORD

It's rare to witness the complete metamorphosis of a person. But over the 25 years I've known Faye, I've watched as she's travelled, honed, collected, distilled, and curated... gradually unfurling into the force she is today.

Even as a teenager, she had a visceral passion for style. While the rest of us were still bumbling about coming to grips with who we were and where we fit in, something flickered within Faye.

Her love of fashion wasn't materialistic or driven by vanity—it was an insatiable quest for the chic in everything. It used all of her senses and lit her up from the inside. Her wardrobe was deliberate and considered, and she pulled it all off with an assured flair not often seen in 18-year-old women.

She and her dad Mick had converted a whole bedroom into a closet. It wasn't the size of it that blew my then tiny, still-developing mind, but the reverence and love she showed for what lay within it. Vintage jackets were treasured, pre-loved boots were savored, tailoring was caressed with a gentle hand. Every piece had a story, which she would tell with sparkling eyes.

Over the years, her nose for style has sharpened and become more discerning—her drive to make a change for the better, laser-focused. That room-sized cupboard has shrunk down to an impossibly small, yet magical space. Through her contagious zeal for sustainable style, Faye shows us all what's possible for the good of our own sense of ourselves and the planet. Not just walking the talk, mind you... but taking great strides with it (in killer thrifted shoes, of course).

Tamara Oudyn, Journalist and Anchor

INTRODUCTION

You Are What You Wear

Imagine a world where our personal style could be of great service.

To support Mother Nature, empower our communities and save the unloved from going to waste.

Thankfully, this isn't a far-away land. Welcome to a long-awaited reality upon us right now and I would love to invite you to share it with me.

It is my intention that in picking up this book, dear reader, you experience a complete fashion perception shift and style *aha moment*, encouraging you towards a totally revolutionary way of thinking.

Just as I have experienced.

A former more-is-more fashion girl, I have slowed right down to become an eco-stylist, which basically means I am a stylist with a sustainable and mindful approach. I choose to work exclusively with fashion that is kind and more considerate of our Earth—op shop, thrift or charity store, vintage, DIY, reimagined, ethical, fair trade, swapped and converted second hand chic. For within these genres there is great power, far beyond a cute outfit.

This is fashion that considers its footprint on people and the planet... and wouldn't you agree that a reverence for all life never goes out of style!?

This book will connect you to the core and caring side of clothes and be a thoroughly rewarding journey back to your true style-self. The one without stress, sizing and social expectation. Whether it be to simply step into a thrift store for the first time and 'try it on,' or to completely reinvent your relationship with fashion.

Less will definitely give you more—from your wardrobe to your wellbeing.

I believe I can empower you to lavish in what I have coined:

OPSHOPULENCE

How to make thrift store look like couture

...and save the planet

Finding the opulence in op shop clothing can make your 'catwalk' a catalyst for change. Second hand fashion holds the potential to be a life and style game changer. It certainly has been for me.

Here are just some of the positives.

I have:

- Saved a stack of cash
- Reduced my stress
- Created my one-of-a kind chic factor
- Supported charity
- Connected with community
- Cleared out the cobwebs, leaving space and clarity for everyday elegance
- Expanded my mind, nourished my soul and learnt to let go
- Discovered my purpose
- Scored my dream job
- Found my divine husband, Lee
- Revitalized my health, habits and even my holy matrimony

All while never *ever* having to sacrifice style!

I mean if that's not a case for thrift shopping and the art of Opshopulence then I don't know what is!

When you choose Opshopulence, you don't just give yourself an elevated look, you elevate and empower community too.

The mission of a charity like The Salvation Army exists to support people who are going through some pretty tough stuff—domestic violence, homelessness, drug and alcohol addiction, gambling dependency, and even natural disasters.

While some of these things may seem a world away from you, you'd be surprised what your neighbor is battling with, and when you're really deep in it, it's a very heavy load to know how to shift.

So shopping at your local thrift store enables you to be a force for good and vote with your fashion dollar.

To me, the clothes in thrift stores really are incredible change agents; they are just waiting for a chance to be of service through you. It's style symbiosis, and the way we must move forward... this is future fashion.

#FASHIONREVOLUTION

One garbage truck of textiles is landfilled or incinerated every second.

- ELLEN MACARTHUR FOUNDATION, 2017 -

Another massive pro is that thrift shopping keeps fashion in the loop. What that means is we enable the clothes to continue rolling and being reused in the textile cycle instead of relinquishing them to a life in landfill, which equals waste and a woeful amount of pollutants on our planet.

There's plenty in Opshopulence for you as an individual. Firstly the 'feel goodness' of knowing you can help is pretty great right!? Secondly, in a field of fast-fashion sheep, pre-loved allows you to be the leader of your own herd, promoting creativity, ingenuity, and a chance to develop a unique style story. Very rarely do op shops have multiples of one item, so it presents a fantastic opportunity for individual quirk and fashion insouciance.

All the mainstream retail rules go out the window—size, section, perception, and our insatiable quest for perfection. Op shopping allows you to play and develop a look intrinsic to you.

Seriously, it's good stuff this slow-fashion game.

> 'If it's a piece of fabric, I listen to the threads.
> It's not intellectual at all. The price is nothing.
> It's the emotional content I have to feel it in my gut.
> I don't know how to explain it other than that.'
>
> Iris Apfel, *Vogue* April 2015

> 'I don't really shop unless its thrift.'
>
> Jeremy Scott, Creative Director, Moschino

> 'That's what fascinates me about period clothes,
> old clothes, costume and charity shop finds,
> that they come imbued with the emotion of the
> wearer—well that for me is just heaven.'
>
> John Galliano, Creative Director, Maison Margiela

Opshopulence is a shape-shifter—a stylish, yet simple insider's guide to elevating your look, your life and the life of others.

I will highlight the profound connection between community, consciousness, caring for the planet yet still looking incredibly chic.

I want to remind you that you can be abundant regardless of your bank balance.

How fabulous it will feel to stand for something much deeper than a season 'must have'.

Side Note: I am not a traditional stylist, and this is not a traditional book about styling. If you want to know how to dress for your pear, apple or banana body shape, I suggest you go to the farmer's market!

20 THINGS WE SHOULD ALL STOP WEARING...

1-20

THE WEIGHT OF OTHER PEOPLE'S EXPECTATIONS

I care less about what you actually wear and more about:

- Does it make you feel fantastic?
- Is it fashion focused on being a force for good?

Because this is a look that never goes out of style

I mean, why do I have to be boxed in by what kind of fruit I am, can't I just be me!? I have chosen to be guided by my fashion feel and style intuition, and I invite you to do the same.

Having said that, I will show you how to look seriously eco-chic no matter your age, size or shape. PLUS how to honor who you are and add in one-of-a-kind style accents that say *I have arrived!*

EVERY YEAR, WOMEN IN AUSTRALIA BUY 27 KILOS OF CLOTHING ONLY TO DISCARD 23

textilebeat.com

Thanks to digital media, we are placing incredible pressure on ourselves to have the latest and greatest, with many young girls admitting to the stress of—heaven forbid—being seen in the same outfit *twice*.

According to research by environmental charity Hubbub, 41% of all 18-25-year-olds feel the pressure to wear a different outfit every time they go out, rising to 47% for young women. One in six young people even say they don't feel they can wear an outfit again once it's been worn on social media.

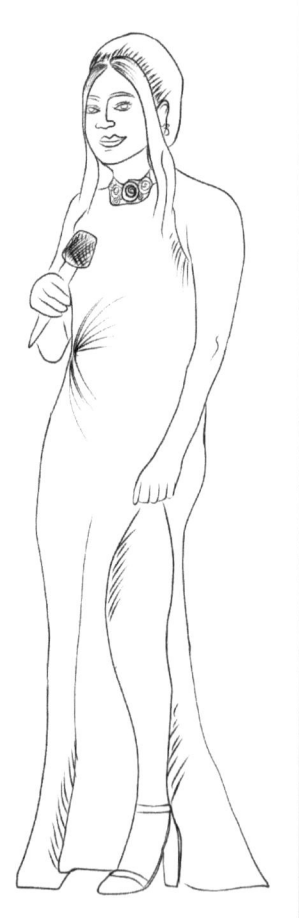

'I know this girl that goes to private school— she's not rich, she's going on a scholarship and kids make fun of her if she's wearing the same jacket after three days. When she saw me in the McQueen dress, she hit me up. She said it made her feel so good to see that I was wearing the same dress when people make fun of her and are like, "Girl, you got the same jacket on." She's like "I'm Tiffany Haddish today."'

Tiffany Haddish, Hollywood actress and A-game outfit repeater

We have a designer and high-street deficit—broke, burnt out, and a cupboard bursting with copious amounts of clothes we don't even wear. The insatiable style beast is stressing, stretching, and sending us into a spin. Seriously, who is the show even for?

Thankfully, there is a better way, and a conscious wardrobe is the change agent—elevating how we feel, the effect we can have on others as well as the world around us. Yes, fashion can be that powerful and it's an opshopportunity for me as an eco-stylist to foster a new fashion breed. The old and forgotten is fabulously reincarnated into a **new to me** high-end muse.

There is much beauty to be found in the underdog.

It starts with how we see the second hand economy, taking pride in pre-loved can be a profound transformation.

To paraphrase the late great Wayne Dyer:

I believe, that abundance is not something we acquire but something we become.

It is the foundation for a truly decadent way to live. Opshopulence is only a thought and a thrifted outfit away.

Opshopulence is a kinder way to be cute.

It's time to redefine the real meaning of fashion luxury.

Welcome to the re-wear renaissance!

A Re-fashioned Fairytale

Imagine this...

She strolls in, and the whole room stops to stare. This woman has an energy.

Expensive fills the air. The shoulders on her fine-wool suit jacket are so sharp I swear (on Chanel) you could slice bread with them, and trimmed with amazing brass buttons—they are the star upon an already super chic Christmas tree.

In a clearly pro move, she ever so nonchalantly teamed this slick tailoring with a simple white t-shirt and relaxed vintage denim. This lady was rocking the kind of dichotomy style dreams are made of. Suede pointy-toe stilettos stepped her into French magazine editor status instantly.

On her decolletage, a collection of carefully curated and layered fine-gold pendants, designer trinkets from her travels perhaps? She carried a beautiful, black leather bamboo-handled bag, gold embossed with her initials. Surely, vintage Gucci.

A bold red lip sealed the sass deal.

Seriously, she waltzed around that room like she owned it and looked like she could afford it too. However, this heartbreakingly chic woman holds a secret. Something so shocking you may find it hard to believe at first...

Her entire outfit cost $50!!

The woman I'm describing is me, and my darling, it can easily be you.

Catch your breath and let me break it down for you.

The ensemble is 100% thrifted and then thoughtfully elevated to a new kind of luxe:

- Plastic buttons replaced with vintage brass offerings
- The magic of contrasting clothing textures—classic staples meets sharp tailoring for a striking appeal
- A statement power heel
- Pre-loved leather bag with beautiful designer accents, personalized with embossed initials by a local family-owned boot maker
- Necklaces are up-cycled, and collected over time—Chanel, Gucci and LV buttons—a slice of designer for less from **@shopportunityvintage**

This, my friends, is the fine art of refashioning thrift. Remastering, reinventing and reshaping pre-loved perceptions.

This is
OPSHOPULENCE

OPSHOPULENCE

:/noun

How to make thrift store
look like couture

… and save the planet

'Her outfit was spectacularly Opshopulent.'

Also see:
Shape-shifting second hand clothing into first class chic

Bad and Boujee

> 'My love of vintage clothing sustained me on a budget. Thank you, Salvation Army and the Rose Bowl Flea Market. Second hand clothing helped me understand that style has nothing to do with money. It's the way you put things together. Style is the HOW not the WHAT.'
>
> Tracee Ellis Ross
>
> 'Style is the only thing you can't buy. It's not in a shopping bag, label, or price tag, it's something reflected from our soul to the outside world —an emotion.'
>
> Alber Elbaz

Being Opshopulent is a mindset, it's a lifestyle. A state of Opshopulence allows you to lavish yourself with pride and pretty no matter the pennies you have. This is a way of living that is better for people and the planet.

Remember: just because you don't have a princess-worthy budget doesn't mean you can't feel like one. Incidentally, I think what makes a true princess is compassion. You see, looking expensive has nothing to do with a big bank account or branded labels.

It's all about preparation meeting opshop-portunity!

Let me give you an example. I spent my childhood watching my mum, Nadia, shift the way I saw beauty. She didn't grow up with much, so she developed this otherworldly ability to find magic in the forgotten—deconstructing, DIY'ing and re-designing the drab into seriously fab. Following her innate gift and her eco-goddess given talent, Mum filled my formative years with incredible creativity which, in looking back, was based around making do, mending, and bending perceptions. Unintentionally she was teaching me to do the same, and so began my eco-education, with Mum as the ultimate mindfulness muse.

For a long time, this practice was really about play for me: with craft'ernoons a plenty I would watch Mum create ***Vogue for very little***. Refashioning inexpensive charity shop finds into a fully styled scene. Seeing her Cheshire-cat grin at what she had whipped up instilled promise in me too. Without fail, she would *Martha Stewart* something so beautiful out of simple bits and bobs. Every. Single. Time.

However, it wasn't until I was living overseas that this Opshopulent playtime truly became a practicality. Travelling, trying to ironically find my place in the world and on a very tight budget, thrift shopping was genuinely all I could afford, but why did that mean I had to forgo looking stylish!?

Determined to prove this theory wrong, I began crafting my own expression of the wisdom bestowed upon me, refashioning high-end style for minimal spend.

With Mum at the forefront of my thoughts, I could remove judgment of where the clothes came from and focus on my creativity to conjure one-of-a-kind cool.

Enter my dad Mick…

> 'Style is pretty much everything to me. I think it's incredibly important. It's such a feel-good thing as well, you know? There's no better feeling for a guy to wear a great tailored suit, freshly starched shirt, great shoes… you feel a million dollars. And that's always been my mantra, to always look and feel good.'
>
> Mick De Lanty (my dad)

For as long as I can remember, a considerable stack of *British Vogue* and *The Face* magazines could be found in our house. These style-bibles became my favorite kind of fairy tale, and I truly believe an unplanned sartorial PhD—wising me up about brand DNA, fashion storytelling, fabric, cut, attention to detail, how a garment falls and the way a cuff can sit just so.

More on this later, but both these factors—equal parts Mum and Micky D—definitely equipped me with some serious pre-loved ninja prowess.

Now it's my turn to pass this knowledge onto you.

Throughout this book I will equip you with the same stealthy style ability. I'm excited to give you the confidence, clever secrets, creative tips and cool awakenings to empower you to take your own journey into Opshopulence.

But first, I want to share with you why sustainability isn't just a sexy buzz word.

It has to become a no-brainer for our beautiful planet.

CHAPTER ONE

Why we Need a Fashion Revolution

'There is no beauty in the finest cloth
if it makes hunger and unhappiness.'

Gandhi

On April 24th 2013, 1138 people died and another 2500 were injured when the factory they were working in collapsed. Even though the employees warned the manager about the visible cracks in the walls, they were forced to continue working; and work they did, tirelessly, on terrible pay with absolutely no consideration—or human rights—to create fast-fashion.

For us.

This was the Rana Plaza disaster in Bangladesh, and an overwhelming reason why we need a fashion revolution. The way we produce fashion must change, but first we must change what we inadvertently support.

These are real people making our clothes. Mostly marginalized women of color, their bare hands crafting the garments we wear, and for so long we never thought to question what went on behind the scenes. What was life like for them?

Were they ok? Were they being treated with kindness? Could they even take a lunch break or go to the bathroom? We just grabbed the bargain deals without a second thought. But take the time to reflect and you'll discover that low-price garment saw someone else pay. This 'style steal', in reality, just robs another of basic human rights like food, shelter and sanitation.

> 'The world now consumes about 80 billion new pieces of clothing every year. This is 400% more than the amount we consumed just two decades ago. As new clothing comes into our lives, we also discard it at a shocking pace. The average American now generates 82 pounds of textile waste each year. That adds up to more than 11 million tons of textile waste from the U.S. alone.'
>
> The True Cost movie

Enormity and scale aside, fashion also uses an incredible amount of energy—chemicals and resources to create clothes. Did you know it takes up to 10,000 liters of water to make ONE PAIR of denim jeans!? Cotton is a very thirsty, greedy fiber. It needs water for growth, manufacturing, dyeing, and washing.

> *'We are living in a climate emergency and the fashion and textiles sector is one of the most polluting and wasteful industries. The industry continues to lack transparency, with widespread exploitation of people working in the supply chain. Never before have there been this many people on the planet in slavery, and fashion is a key driver of this reality. Brands and retailers are still not taking enough responsibility for the pay and working conditions in their factories, the environmental impacts of the materials they use or how the products they make affect the health of people, animals and our living planet'.*
>
> Fashion Revolution

Thankfully, two visionary women—Carry Somers and Orsola de Castro—raised the question that really needed to be asked.

#WHOMADEMYCLOTHES

This hashtag hit the global social media highway and Fashion Revolution was born.

Fash Rev has now become the world's largest fashion activism movement. Every year on the anniversary of the Rana Plaza factory collapse, during the week of 19th-25th April, Fashion Revolution encourages millions of people to come together to advocate for systemic change in the fashion industry.

> *'We campaign for a clean, safe, fair, transparent and accountable fashion industry. We do this through research, education, collaboration, mobilization and advocacy. The issues in the fashion industry never fall on any single person, brand, or company. That's why we focus on using our voices to transform the entire system. With systemic and structural change, the fashion industry can lift millions of people out of poverty and provide them with decent and dignified livelihoods. It can conserve and restore our living planet. It can bring people together and be a great source of joy, creativity and expression for individuals and communities. We believe in a global fashion industry that conserves and restores the environment and values people over growth and profit.'*
>
> Fashion Revolution

The movement has been responsible for many brands changing their ways. It has seen them reassessing their production process, reducing their impact on people and the planet but most importantly, putting their hand up and admitting they want to do better and that's a big step!

I spoke with Fashion Revolution co-founder, Carry Somers. Here is a glimpse from our conversation.

FDL: Carry, thank you for all that you do for our beloved Mother Earth. Could we start with a snapshot of how the Fashion Revolution movement, co-founded by you and Orsola, came to be?

CS: Fashion Revolution was founded in the aftermath of the Rana Plaza factory collapse in Bangladesh in 2013 when 1138 died and thousands more were injured. When I saw activists physically searching through the rubble to prove which brands were producing there, it was evident that the fashion industry needed revolutionary change. Over time, the crazy idea I had in the bath one day grew to the world's largest fashion activism movement. We now have teams in almost 100 countries around the world and work all year round to mobilize citizens, industry and policy makers through our research, education and advocacy work.

FDL: It's absolutely incredible to see the traction Fashion Revolution has had, the momentum and change created. I would love to know some of your most proud shape-shifting moments with the movement thus far?

CS: Every time I look at social media and see photographs of people holding #imadeyourclothes posters, I feel very proud to have helped provide visibility for the stories of the weavers, dyers, embroiderers, cotton farmers, seamstresses, spinners, union leaders and all the other people who make our clothing and accessories around the world.

Catch our chat in full, Chapter 13.

Fashion Revolution Week is a wonderful opportunity to speak up for a sustainable fashion industry and it's really easy to get involved. Reach out to brands and ask them **#whomademyclothes** as well as #**whatsinmyclothes**.

Explore these Fash Rev hashtags, as well as #**haulternative** or write a sartorial love story.

The Fashion Revolution website is an invaluable resource, and I highly recommend getting woke and exploring it! There's loads of advice, facts, stats, and case studies to educate yourself.

www.fashionrevolution.org

And you don't have to wait for Fashion Revolution Week to come around; we need a Fashion Revolution every day!

Connect with the community, be curious and committed to change. Never underestimate the vast difference your voice can make. When we all sing the same universal fashion song, it's powerful.

> *'My feminism was the reason I stopped supporting fast-fashion in the first place. Around 80% of garment workers are women and they are often incredibly underpaid and working in dangerous conditions. Many face sexual harassment in their workplaces and are unable to unionize protest. It's also a race issue because the majority of garment workers are black and brown women—and that is the integral reason as to why this has been allowed to happen and continues to happen.'*
>
> Josephine Philips, Sojo app

So much of what goes on behind the scenes, the lack of ethics or sustainability, we are not able to see on the price tag. The V&A (Victoria and Albert Museum, London) also has some great resources around the impact of the fashion industry. According to the V&A:

Ethical Fashion aims to address the problems it sees with the way the fashion industry currently operates, such as exploitative labor, environmental damage, the use of hazardous chemicals, waste, and animal cruelty.

- *Serious concerns are often raised about exploitative working conditions in the factories that make cheap clothes for the high-street.*
- *Child workers, alongside exploited adults, can be subjected to violence and abuse such as forced overtime, as well as cramped and unhygienic surroundings, bad food, and very poor pay. The low cost of clothes on the high-street means that less and less money goes to the people who actually make them.*
- *Cotton provides much of the world's fabric, but growing it uses 22.5% of the world's insecticides and 10% of the world's pesticides, chemicals which can be dangerous for the environment and harmful to the farmers who grow it (Ethical Fashion Forum).*
- *Current textile growing practices are considered unsustainable because of the damage they do to the immediate environment. For example, the Aral Sea in Central Asia has shrunk to just 15% of its former volume, largely due to the vast quantity of water required for cotton production and dyeing (Ethical Fashion Forum).*

- *Most textiles are treated with chemicals to soften and dye them, however these chemicals can be toxic to the environment and can be transferred to the skin of the people wearing them. Hazardous chemicals used commonly in the textile industry are: lead, nickel, chromium IV, aryl amines, phthalates and formaldehyde (Greenpeace).*
- *The low costs and disposable nature of high-street fashion means that much of it is destined for incinerators or landfill sites. The UK alone throws away one million tons of clothing every year (Waste Online).*
- *Many animals are farmed to supply fur for the fashion industry, and many people feel that their welfare is an important part of the Ethical Fashion debate. The designer Stella McCartney uses neither fur nor leather in her designs. In an advert for the animal rights organization, PETA, she said: 'we address... ethical or ecological... questions in every other part of our lives except fashion.'*

www.vam.ac.uk

'I just hope that the consumer realizes their full potential and their full power. It's going to be very scary when the consumer finally wakes up and says: you know what, I don't need any of this. I can make it myself, I can buy vintage… we just want the consumer to continue to exercise their power.'

Ali Richmond, Fashion For All.

1 NO POVERTY

2 ZERO HUNGER

3 GOOD HEALTH AND WELL-BEING

4 QUALITY EDUCATION

5 GENDER EQUALITY

6 CLEAN WATER AND SANITATION

SDG artists impression by @thriftwithindi

This illustration is a glimpse of the '17 Sustainable Development Goals' as set by the United Nations, including crucial elements such as no poverty, no hunger, gender equality, reduced inequalities, responsible consumption and production.

Indi has illustrated the first six for us, however please head to the United Nations website to dive into each goal in more detail, and to see the vision and what has been achieved so far. Indi's illustration of their official graph is a great visual to keep at hand. This is what we want the brands we support to stand for.

I think the other element to really ponder is our disconnection to our clothes; in my opinion, it is fast-fashion that has created the sartorial separation. The time, thought, and sentiment of our grandparents', even our parents' style era have been replaced with quick fixes and unfinished seams. When things are so cheap and attainable, value is cast aside. We don't have to wait, so why would we care? But the crazy thing is, it ends up costing you more in the long run because fast-fashion is designed for obsolescence.

You'll know if you've ever bought a 'bargain' because as fast as the fashion itself, buttons fall off, garments lose their shape, stitching unravels... it's so not worth it for yourself, the poor soul who made it, nor Mother Earth.

> 'Fast-fashion is like fast food.
> After the sugar rush it just leaves
> a bad taste in your mouth.'
> Livia Firth, Founder and Creative Director, ECO AGE

Within this fast-paced way we have also lost connection to community and artisan culture, not to mention inclusivity and diversity. There is so much wisdom and beauty to be found within our native cultures. Take my home, Australia, and its incredible indigenous people, their messages, the language of the land, country and story or Dreaming is so divine.

First Nations Fashion

I would like to acknowledge the traditional owners of country throughout Australia. We pay our respects to them. Their cultures, their ancestors, their elders. We respect and honor their sacred wisdom and knowledge.

SUE-ANNE HUNTER, A WURUNDJERI AND NGURAI ILLUM WURRING WOMAN

'A woman armed with ancestral wisdom is an unstoppable force.'

Sue-Anne Hunter, a proud Wurundjeri woman, works as a First Nations consultant and finds great courage and strength from wearing her culture. Earrings are a big form of expression for Sue-Anne; she sports bling featuring her creator, Bunjil, her people's flag and indigenous elements like feathers and native animals all displaying her story through style.

Sue-Anne advocates tirelessly to shift perceptions, and fights to have her people heard. Her young daughter, Jedda, is a powerful next-generation First Nations young woman, embodying her mum's warrior spirit.

This is Sue-Anne's and Jedda's creation story
as told by her uncle, Ian Hunter.

BUNJIL AND HIS FLIGHT TO THE STARS

'Bunjil, our god, the eagle... he came from the sun and created all the living things. He created the Wurundjeri people of the Kulin Nation, the land and all the creatures that lived on it.

Creation, that made Bunjil tired, so he rested and proudly overlooked his beautiful land and its beings. Then Bunjil was tired of Earth so Bunjil asked Ballan Ballan, the crow, keeper of the winds to release them from his bag to create a whirlwind to take Bunjil and his family high, high up into the heavens.

A whirlwind started and trees blew but not enough for Bunjil. He called on Ballan Ballan to open his bag wider, so Ballan Ballan did, and this released an almighty wind. Bunjil told his sons to join him too, so the hawks, the little possums and the parakeets jumped into the wind and away they were taken high up into the heavens, 'round and 'round they went, high up into the sky.

Today Bunjil and his sons all watch over the Wurundjeri people and the Kulin Nation as stars.

This story has been passed down over hundreds of years from elder to child. It was told to me when I was a little fella and now, I give this story to you.

So next time you gaze up into the night sky, look for Bunjil watching over us and nearby his sons making up the stars of the Southern Cross that help guide us and the Kulin Nation people home.'

It's just so beautiful, isn't it?

Whether you be Australian, American, or Polynesian like my husband, take the time to explore the native culture that surrounds you and the country in which you reside. Educate yourself, help elevate and empower, always come from kindness and share your learnings with your community. Wisdom is a powerful catalyst for change. There are so many sublime stories of culture that can be found in fashion, be sure to check out the resource below to discover more about First Nations Fashion.

First Nations Fashion and Design
firstnationsfashiondesign.com
Instagram @first.nations.fashion.design

Quality Time

Quality is always better than quantity and we can equip ourselves with sound knowledge for making more informed choices.

Here is some great advice from a favorite Instagram account of mine @**project_stopshop**

> Key features to consider when checking the quality of a garment, either in a store or within the walls of your own wardrobe, is to turn them inside out and investigate:
>
> - Are the edges and hems of the fabric finished well? Loose threads could snag and cause fraying.
> - Count the stitches per inch—more stitches mean more time's been spent making the garment, and more care and attention in making the garment durable.
> - Any additional items such as buttons and zips should be securely attached in place. These get a lot of use and need to be hard wearing.
> - Cut on the bias versus cut on the grain. Bias cut means cutting the fabric at a 43-degree angle so that it will drape nicely, contour to the shape of the body, and give you a beautiful twirl when you move. This is more expensive and time consuming to do. A cheaper, mass-produced garment would be cut on the grain, which means it is done straight on running fabric and doesn't hang anywhere near as nicely as the bias cut.
> - Quality inside and out. Take a peek at the underbelly of the garment for more intel. Are the seams finished beautifully? Threads all intact? How's the stitching? What does the lining look and feel like?

Quality over quantity may at times cost more of a premium but it's this purpose-driven purchase that supports planet and people, and gives our clothes the power to make change. Now you know what to look for, be sure to keep an eye out for those special pieces and garment details in thrift stores, especially on vintage, designer and handmade items!

The Repair Revolution

'Luxury is that which
you can repair.'

Grandfather of Hermès, artistic director,
Pierre-Alexix Dumas

'The old expression holds that a well repaired object can be 'as good as new.' Today I'd argue that this no longer applies, because in 2021, a well repaired object isn't as good as new, it's better. The rise of conspicuous non-consumption has been a long time coming.

Over the last decade or so, we have witnessed a slow and sometimes painful pivot as fashion at first ignored, then loftily entertained and finally fell head over heels for the concert of sustainability. Those who were once dismissed as sack-wearing, soy-munching, gaia-loving outliers—ideology-driven pioneers such as before-her-time Katherine Hamnett, perfectly-timed Stella McCartney and of-his-time Christopher Raeburn—have proven to be the Cassandras who first saw what most fashion was too busy making new stuff to realize. As a marker of desirability, being environmentally virtuous has transitioned from niche consideration to central parameter of desire. To succeed commercially, fashion must reflect and service the desires of its times. Which is why at a time when it has dawned on many of us that the Paris Agreement (on Climate Change) is far more significant than Paris Fashion week.'

Luke Leitch, Vogue.com

These words by Luke Leitch on **Vogue.com** really resonated with me. The whole Opshopulence concept came to light for me over 10 years ago and for quite a while, most thought I was that soy-munching gaia-loving outlier he mentions. While I do happen to love both these things, I was hell-bent on changing the narrative and perception of second hand. The time has definitely come where it is now cool, and completely essential might I add.

> 'The U.S. second hand clothes market
> is projected to grow from $28 billion
> in 2019 to $64 billion in 2024.'
>
> Thredup, online thrift portal

Shopping second hand keeps our fashion in the loop; we allow it to continue rotating by finding new ways to love it all over again. Whether it be thrifting, reselling or vintage, for me these clothes have character and they're the kinds of friends you want long term.

> 'We shouldn't be measuring a garment's value
> by its price tag, but by the purpose it has in our life.
> We should own it because we love it, and because
> we love it we should want to keep it for ever.'
>
> Orsola de Castro, Loved Clothes Last

I fondly recall my grandma repairing her clothes and mine, in fact it was Dorothy Fay who equipped me with my needle and thread know-how. Having the ability to retain our clothing and accessories does indeed invoke that wonderful feeling, especially when the item carries a significant memory or emotion special to you.

Don't Despair...
Repair!

The story behind my vintage handbag rescue

I try not to get too attached to material things these days but oh my, the thought of losing my beautiful vintage leather and bamboo bag was a tough one. You see, we met when I first began my beloved role as eco-stylist for Salvos Stores in 2015. It was like she was waiting for me in all her designer-inspired glory to confirm my deep-seated belief that second hand could be seriously chic and I could create a purpose-driven job around such a knowing.

Back then, sustainable style certainly wasn't a hot topic like it is now. In fact a lot of people thought I was a little nuts, but I persisted with my vision for a world where second hand could be transformed into first-class chic. Thankfully, the Salvos could see it too and so we began our journey together, bringing awareness to conscious style.

This bag came with me to many a meeting as we crafted the concept of eco-styling our stores. She supported me on my very first op shop event, Salvos thrift boutique opening and even our fledgling morning televsion alliance. She's elevated an enormous amount of my ensembles and stopped many a stylista in their tracks to salivate over her Gucci-esque vibes.

Despite her $10 price tag, she looks a million bucks to me. Carrying her always makes me feel fancy, a one-of-a-kind cool. She is proof that it's really not about the label, and I love her for that.

So you can imagine how my heart dropped when her cute little bamboo clasp came apart, ironically at an eco-fashion event. I visited every boot maker in town; sadly they all told me her time had come. I wasn't having it. There had to be a way to save her from the scrap heap.

Determined to get my don't despair, repair on, I refused to stop until I found a solution.

Not just for sustainability's sake, which of course is a huge driving force for me, but because I genuinely love her too.

Praise be to my pre-loved tenacity and the Google fashion gods, I finally discovered Sole Heeled. Seriously, they saved my second hand life.

Mark and the team were incredibly helpful and understanding, and really went above and beyond to help me. My bag wasn't easy, taking us a little bit of back and forth to get it sorted but they stayed with it instead of saying it was too hard like all the other boot makers and repair merchants. I am so happy to be back with this beauty.

By repairing, we are keeping our beloved accessories in the loop and out of landfill.

Now that's a love story if you ask me.

Discover my Louis Vuitton bag rescue and reinvention with local craftswoman Lene Smit.

@fayedelanty

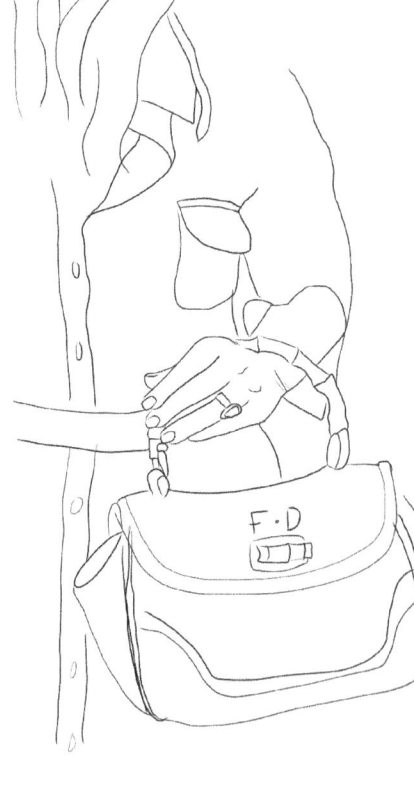

Many brands are building the repair model into their manifestos. Nudie Jeans now train all their staff in the merits of the make-do and mend mindset for patching, restitching, and salvation of your favorite distressed denim from their namesake.

So if you have a pair of Nudie jeans that need some lovin', you can take them to any Nudie Jeans store or 'Repair Stores', as they are known and get them restitched and ready for business. For free. No matter where you bought them!

Check out their book, *Start your own f*cking brand*, written by Nudie co-founder Maria Erixon, for a behind the scenes look at this iconic eco empire.

> *'Around two years ago now, I made the conscious move away from fast-fashion because I became aware of how, as an industry, it was exploiting women of color. I decided to stop supporting brands that had built their successes off a supply chain that violated human rights, and in doing so I started finding other ways to consume fashion. I was a student, so I found that second hand clothes were the perfect mix of sustainable and affordable. But there was one problem—whether in charity shops, thrift stores or on Depop, I'd constantly find clothes that I loved that weren't my size. I realized the solution was to alter the clothes to fit me... but I didn't know how to sew and going to a seamster was too much time and effort. So really it was out of personal need—I wanted something that would make clothing alterations and repairs incredibly easy in that all you have to do is book it on your phone and then the rest would be taken care of. And from that, Sojo was born!'*
>
> Josephine Phillips, SOJO app founder

Beautiful, sustainable brand Brunello Cucinelli, uses a sartorial light language speaking of never-ending stories, simplicity and the concept of infinity for our clothes, even sighting a new social contract with creation. Once you purchase an item from Brunelli, all subsequent repairs are free, essentially offering a life-time of wear from one of his garments.

'Our mothers taught us that the art of darning and mending highlights the value of things. John Ruskin used to say that while we must necessarily accept the end of the objects we use, still we must do our best to make them last longer. This is precisely the purpose of mending, and in our company, we have a specific department devoted to it.'

Brunello Cucinelli

I also adore the Instagram of heritage British brand, Trickers, who have been resoling and repairing shoes since 1829. Every Thursday, **@trickers_shoes** highlight a customer repair success story. They have over 100 overhaul undertakings each month. The oldest pair they have worked on was over 40 years old. There really isn't a pair Trickers can't fix! Ironically, their eco-ethos is creating an infinitely lighter footprint.

Do some investigating yourself and see who's in your 'hood. Support small businesses and in turn support the circular economy.

'When you buy from a small business an actual person does a little happy dance!'

I also have a great bootmaker who has re-soled all of our shoes, including my husband's beloved snakeskin converse he bought when we first started dating, and thanks to Mario they are still going strong.

His business has been in the family for over 30 years, as has Lucy—my local embroidery lady—who adds the most amazing personal touches to my thrift finds.

My neighbor and now dear friend, Jan, is my tailor and dressmaker on speed dial, reworking my wardrobe when it wears thin, fixing my husband's over-loved shorts time and time again and even indulging me in designer recreations using items I find at op shops.

As Orsola de Castro says, 'The joy of rewearing and repairing our clothes can be a revolutionary act'. Be sure to explore her beautiful book *Loved Clothes Last* for further make do and mend inspiration.

There is just so much we can do with what we already have.

However, what happens when what we do have isn't making us feel good?

Style not size • Love the skin you're in • Self love is a super power •

Post-Traumatic DRESS Disorder

> 'Stop cutting the fabric of your soul
> into pieces to clothe other people.'
>
> Nikita Gill

This great quote got me thinking, not just about the disposable nature of fashion, but of life and relationships too. How often do we forgo our values to validate another? Hold off on speaking our mind for fear of offending? This was certainly the case for me for quite a while—wearing all the latest and greatest in an attempt to impress, yet it never really made me happy, certainly not my bank account either.

I was a walking, talking 'well dressed' product of this insatiable machine, freely feeding the beast that should have been starving. Instead, I was hungry to fit in and suffering from what I like to call: Post-Traumatic DRESS Disorder (PTDD).

I thought when I slowed down, my fast 'fashion crises' would come to an end. It had been years, but my most recent and unexpected expression hit me hard. You know the ones when you get whipped into an 'I hate everything I own' frenzy? I look fat in it all, it's too hot, I can't cope, and discombobulation ensues. I used to get these a lot in my twenties when I was definitely dressing to impress, so it was an unwelcome surprise for myself and my poor husband when this one really dug its judgmental little claws in. It's like a dark fashion wave that you can't seem to swim your way out of, an all-encompassing ocean of ickiness.

Apparently, a minimalist closet doesn't necessarily prevent a to-the-max flip out when it comes to picking what to wear, especially if you're feeling a little unseasonal. The simple act of going out for ice cream one balmy evening turned into an emotional wardrobe war zone. After a tense twenty minutes, thankfully my beloved Lee found the strength to hold the space and ask me what was really going on.

'This isn't really about the dress, is it, babe?'

Boom!!!

The simplest of questions for the most complex concern... albeit completely irrational on my part.

My heaven-sent husband helped me realize it had absolutely nothing to do with the clothes and everything to do with the inner me. I was having an epic girl moment of insecurity. I believe this self-induced condition is the flow-on effect of the insatiable fast-fashion beast. PTDD is a toxic ailment that messes with our logical mind and makes us overreact, all in the name of an outfit. The resounding symptom? Extreme sartorial stress from striving to fit in. Y'all feel me?

*Side note: Post Traumatic DRESS Disorder is an impossible and pointless roundabout that's hard to exit, so it's best to ease up on yourself, *people!*

But in the thick of it, it's really hard to see that. Every woman I've spoken to while writing this—including my friends, followers, and neighbors—all wholeheartedly relate they've been through it and it can be one hell of a heavy energy. Especially during Australian summers when everything is harder! For me it's definitely reflective of what I'm going through or feeling about myself at the time, and when PTDD strikes I know I'm struggling with something deeper than how a skirt fits. Over the last year I've been growing into a new fashion form; my body has changed. My mindset, perceptions and preferences have also changed, and I'm having sartorial teething problems! I wasn't being real about that with myself, so it had to come out in another way. Hello PTDD! I see now how much our emotional state is woven into our wardrobes.

> 'You need to learn how to select your thoughts just the same way you select your clothes every day. This is a power you can cultivate.'
>
> Elizabeth Gilbert, *Eat Pray Love*

Sometimes it can be hard to let go, especially when it comes to style. Our clothes collect memories of special or stressful times in our lives. A first date, a new job, a break-up, a break *through* or a fresh start but sometimes they can hold us back too.

Enter the *'I'll fit in to it agains'* and the *'Maybe I'll wear them down the trackies'*... aka dust gatherers and closet stuffer upper'ers.

These pieces connect us to a happy or sad time and either way it can leave us feeling stuck, trying to tap back into or reluctantly move past the way things *wore*. Clothes really can elevate or make us hibernate!

When I was living overseas and travelling to ironically find my place in the world, I spent a lot of time living out of a suitcase, so I was forced to adopt the mantra of less is more. Let me tell you, for a past life *more is more* lady, that was terrifying! Especially when I could no longer afford all the 'pretty things.' I'd placed my importance into how I was perceived, and it was a big learning curve. I recently read about *the spotlight effect*[1], which refers to the tendency of thinking more people notice something about you than they actually do. Like 'gee you look bloated today,' 'ewww you have a stain on your collar' or 'wow she is so last season.' Guess what? For the most part we grossly overestimate it.

However, when you're trapped in that emotional hole and not really digging what you are wearing, worrying too much what others think, or we aren't being our own best friend, then everything gets blown way out of proportion. Basically, it's our egocentrism that causes it; we see the world from the center of our own universe. It's not to say we are arrogant, it's just that we see things from our own experience and therein lies the problem.

The funny thing is, everyone else is doing the same thing in their own mini universe. Now I'm no psychiatrist but that makes perfect sense to me.

Social media such as Instagram and Tik Tok plays a big part in skewing our view too. Everyone's 'highlight reel' is actually so unreal that it messes with our self-image. Especially when we met three girls from the ABC's War on Waste series (Australia), who said they would be mortified if their followers saw them in the same outfit twice. Is this the lifecycle of our style evolution though? The teens and twenties are a pressure-cooker time to appear cool to our peers. It's kinda primal in a way; we're all subliminally hunting for a mate. Or does the high-street just feed that fashion wolf even further by pumping out new collections every week and enticing the uncertain, searching side of us to buy buy buy!

> 'Part of my mission is to inspire other young people to find themselves in their style and wear what makes them happy. I'm not here to be like everyone else. I'm here to be Indi.'
>
> Indi Field, next generational thrifter @thriftwithindi

I certainly fall prey to the marathon scroll from time to time and while it can be inspiring to a point, eventually all it really does is hurt my wrists and my confidence. Comparison-itis ensues. Even though social media can be incredible for building community, sharing with like-minded people and utilizing the power of free marketing—it has been vital with my work and I'm so grateful for the wonderful community I have supporting me—I do still get whipped up into information overload.

I don't know about you but I'm craving more SOUL-cial media. I've tried to set some healthy boundaries so I don't get stuck in a digital vortex. Here's what I do:

1. I have a preset on my Instagram that gives me a 1.5-hour limit every day. If I go over, I get an alert that pops up on my screen. Most of the time that's enough for the guilts to kick in and make me stop scrolling.
2. Technical sundown alert—at 8:30pm every night, my phone dims her lights and encourages me to down tools.

3. Exercise. I leave my phone at home and take a walk or head to bikram yoga.
4. Practice being present. Making a pot of tea and talking about the day with my hubby or tending to my plants always helps me to switch off. Meditation is amazing too.
5. Go live my life! See a movie, soak up some vitamin D, hit a thrift store, read, take on a DIY project, spend time with my friends.

Upon the uncovering of PTDD, I searched for photos of me wearing dresses in different stages and times of my life. With a small collection in hand I took some time to reflect and make a note of how I was feeling when I was wearing each one. Some fascinating observations arose. Try doing the same and see how you feel.

This is not to say, however, that fashion can't be a force for good and a fabulous form of self-expression. It has the ability to help, heal, empower and totally transform. Those are the kind of clothes I want on my back. I'm just slowly learning to not be a slave by doing more with less, minus the image stress—and you can too.

FOLLOW MY FAIL-PROOF FASHION PRESCRIPTION FOR COMBATING THAT PESKY PTDD...

1. Self love

Speak sweetly to yourself, treat yourself with kindness, do something every day that brings you joy and builds your confidence. For me that's meditation, having a good sweat via bikram yoga, weights or running, being creative, op shopping and practicing gratitude. I like to write a list or vocalize five things I'm thankful for every day. Lee and I quite often do this profound little exercise together; it's a great attitude check!

Emily @Ekoluv

2. Look outside yourself

Awareness is the first step in stopping the insatiable fast-fashion beast. Remind yourself that for the most part no one is even noticing if you've worn the same thing twice. In fact, I'm all about the **#outfitrepeat**. Search the hashtag and find the tribe. It's not only cool but common sense to recycle your ensembles.

> 'I was born before fast-fashion. When I was a student and when I started working, we didn't have fast-fashion and yet I managed to get dressed in a nice way. I just invested in pieces which were good quality and would last a long time in my wardrobe. Call it 'Eco-fashion' if you like, but I think it's just common sense.'
>
> Livia Firth, founder and creative director, Eco Age #30wears

Hey, if it's good enough for Princess Kate and Meghan Markle to wear the same thing more than once, then why can't we!?

3. Do something sweet for another

A thoughtful note or message, a compliment or smile, open the door for someone, help a stranger with their heavy bags, pay it forward and buy the coffee for the person behind you. Remember what's truly of value—family, friends, laughter, loyalty and being a good-hearted person. Kindness is a currency.

> 'There's an outfit for everyday, every occasion. My mind, my brain is always putting together outfits. It's like a meditation. It's my art.'
>
> @stylecrone

'There is something so powerful in confidence around self that makes fashion so powerful, like I think all the time I can do anything if I like how I look; I could start a movement if I like how I look. If I feel my truest self, I'll speak more articulately, more powerfully. So I think the ability to adorn everyone of all walks of life, I think is a really critical role that fashion plays.'

Kimberley Drew, activist and critical thinker

4. Declutter

Get clear on what you do and don't wear. Really dive into how each piece makes you feel and be honest about whether it's elevating you or making you hibernate. Trust me, I totally understand how that can happen.

I'd been hanging onto a few things that were definitely holding me back—skinny jeans that made me feel anything but, fabrics which pulled and restricted me, all because it's what I used to wear and I wasn't willing to let go of 'that girl.' However, once I cut the sartorial cord it created profound fresh-fashion energy.

5. Let go

In my experience, letting go of what no longer serves me has always been an invitation to the universe to bring me more of what I truly need—clarity, abundance, opportunity, and new ideas.

Keen to Marie Kondo yourself now?

'When we really dive into the reasons for why we can't let something go there are only two: an attachment to the past or a fear for the future.'

Marie Kondo, *The Life-changing Magic of Tidying Up*

Wardrobe Wellbeing Cleanse

DIVIDE AND CONQUER

I take absolutely everything out of my wardrobe and put it all on the floor in the lounge room. Not going to lie, this is confronting! Firstly, because you see how much stuff you really do have, and then because you have to figure out whether you want to keep it. You know what, though? It also makes you kind of get the sh**s with yourself, and I found it actually helped build strength for the culling process. It made me crave clarity, and it was exactly the shock I needed to get it done!

COMPARTMENTALIZE

In summer, I gathered all my heavy winter jackets and put them aside. Before I embarked on this process, they were taking up the bulk of my wardrobe and it was making getting dressed in the morning so confusing and uninspiring for me. I couldn't see what I actually wanted to wear or what was relevant for the weather. I assessed my wardrobe space and decided to neatly fold the winter jackets and demote them to the lowest, least accessible shelf. Then the season relevant pieces could take pride of place.

THE HARD QUESTIONS

Yep, it's time to ask them my friends. Consider these:

- What do I wear the most and why?
- When was the last time I wore this? (Season appropriate aside, if it's been four months or more, my rule is it has to go)
- Do I wear this garment, or does it wear me? By that I mean, do you feel yourself when you're in it or do you fuss and fidget?
- Is this piece functional for my lifestyle and my day-to-day sartorial needs?
- Does it bring me joy and make me feel great about myself?
- Would I wear if it I had it mended, customized or altered?

DONATE

Once you've answered those questions truthfully, create a pile of what you know you aren't wearing and prepare them for donation. Passing on good quality pre-loved clothing is a great way to support charity, empower your local community, keep clothing in the fashion loop and away from landfill.

3 EASY WAYS TO DONATE WITH CONSCIOUSNESS

1. **Drop off** to your nearest thrift store during opening hours and give to a staff member or leave in the designated donations area.
2. In Australia, Salvos Stores have a **free collection home service.** There is a form online to apply and book. They also have a downloadable donation guide for each Australian state and an online donation portal. See www.salvosstores.com.au.
3. **Call** a store and chat to the staff, especially if you are unsure about your specific donation.

RE-LOVE

Instead of donating good quality items, you can also consider:

Reselling: via eBay. Etsy, Gumtree, Depop or Poshmark, for example.

Swapping: either via organized swapping events or within your community.

Consignment: selling in a second hand designer store, where the owner receives a portion/cut for hosting your item.

Gifting: to a friend or family member.

Recycle: head to Planet Ark recyclingnearyou.com.au for a great resource on what to do with worn, damaged or unsellable clothing. Alternatively Google recycling centers in your local area.

Upcycle or convert: could you recreate, DIY or redesign an existing piece into something *new to you*?

Either way, these are all great alternatives to clothing ending up in landfill.

> *'When I started my Mary's Living and Giving shops for Save The Children ten years ago, I called it living and GIVING because I wanted us to understand how we're living. When you understand what we are doing as people and how we're choosing to live you understand that the only way back is to be giving. Whether it's donating, or giving time, giving back, recycling. It's the only way we are going to change the world.'*
>
> Mary Portas, *Queen of Shops*

MOVING THE NEEDLE

If you're in Australia, head to: **www.movingtheneedle.com.au**

'Moving the Needle is a really important initiative, in our opinion, which seeks to bring the charity retail sector, retail brands and the customer on a journey together to divert textiles from landfill.'

Aife O'loughlin, customer experience manager, Salvos Stores

Moving the Needle is an opportunity for us all to come together as a collective and shift consciousness, to take action for people and the planet. Meet the two brilliant minds behind the initiative—Edwina and Aife from Salvos Stores, in Chapter 13.

The MTN site helps you find a local donation point near you and also has lots of tips, tricks and resources about textile waste. #reducereuserecycle

If you're overseas, check in with your local charity or thrift store, find out their donation process and partake! Also check your local council, government websites and waste management bodies.

SHOP YOUR WARDROBE

After all the brutality, now it's time to have some fun! Transform your wardrobe into a store worthy incarnation so every time you open it you feel inspired to put outfits together. Neatly fold scarves and t-shirts, iron everything that needs it (saves you time in the long run trust me!). Invest in all white or all wooden hangers. Don't overfill—I've kept my hanger space with a two-finger gap between each piece so I don't feel cluttered and it's a pleasure to shop.

Research clever storage ideas to make your life easier. Pinterest is a gold mine. I'm currently vibing on functional hanging ideas for my scarves and belts so I can create more space in my small wardrobe. Also investigating how I can turn my ever-expanding brooch collection into moveable art!

CONNECT WITH YOUR CLOTHES

Explore op shopping, ethical and vintage fashion. Find ways to connect more to what you put on your body and understand where the garments have come from. Honestly, second hand fashion has gifted me with so much more than just a kind closet, particularly with my mindset. It's massively reduced my PTDD. The things I once viewed as important don't have the pull they used to.

A great resource I use to uncover more about the ethics of brands is: **www.goodonyou.com**

Check out their website or download the app on your phone. You can sign up for free and do your due diligence on labels you are considering shopping with. To add to that, Good On You has some fantastic articles to inspire and educate you along your journey.

The other thing I suggest doing is dive into a brand's website and look for their sustainability page or any info they have about their transparency, ethics, or production values. My rule of thumb is if they don't have one, I would avoid.

You can also harness the power of social media to ask brands more questions and remember the tag **#whomademyclothes** and encourage them to engage and give you more information. If they are responsive, chances are they are aiming to do the right thing.

EMBRACE WHO YOU ARE AND WHERE YOU ARE

Don't try to be the 2005 you. I'm still trying to master this one!

Everyone is different and divine in their own way. Life is about *so* much more than just a dress. But the right dress can reduce your stress, shift your perception, support community, and make you shine far beyond its fabric.

'Good Things Come to Those Who Thrift.'

CHAPTER TWO

Enclothed Cognition
—The science behind style

In 2012 Hajo Adam and Adam D. Galinsky, two professors and psychologists from Bath in England and New York respectively, coined the phrase: 'Enclothed Cognition,' focused on the feel-good factor and power lying within our wardrobes.

Enclothed Cognition refers to the effect clothing has upon a person's mental process and the way they think, feel, and function. I was absolutely thrilled when I discovered this concept within an *Australian Vogue* article *Pieces of Mind* written by Jen Nurick.[2]

It really validated the way I have always seen fashion... as a powerful shape-shifter, mood elevator and catalyst for change. Especially during the year that was 2020, I know for a fact my wardrobe significantly contributed to my wellbeing during COVID lockdown. It became my happy place, play time, an escape even though I couldn't venture much farther than my front door. While isolated, I felt connected thanks to my sustainable fashion community on Instagram who all joined me to dress up despite having nowhere to go. Yep, the THRIFTERHOOD is real! This wardrobe workout, as I like to call it, was even the nudge I needed to write this book you now hold in your hands.

I truly believe the clothing we wear influences our behavior, the way we think and act, and it seems Adam and Gallinsky discovered a resounding yes too.

> *'Interested in the impact our clothing has on our sense of self, the two professors conducted a study where ordinary people were dressed in lab coats and compared their behaviors when they were under the guise of either a doctor or painter. Remarkably, participants who were wearing doctor's garb displayed increased focus and attention compared with those wearing the painter's coat. In addition to finding that we each relate to clothing based on our personal experiences, they also found that when we put on clothes our behaviors and mental state can in fact be altered.'*
>
> Jen Nurick, *Vogue Australia* Nov 2020

While Adam and Galinsky coined the phrase of Enclothed Cognition, the concept of clothing affecting our cognition, how we think and feel, is not new.

Hello activewear making us feel the need to exercise more—well, we live in hope! A great fitting suit bringing the boss and power vibes. I know I always feel my confidence soar in well-cut tailoring. Bright colors can make us feel happy, casual clothes open and agreeable. Lacy underwear can connect us to our divine feminine.[3]

Fashion Psychology is now on the curriculum at the London College of Fashion, spearheaded by Professor Carolyn Mair PhD, behavioral psychologist and author of *The Psychology of Fashion*.

> *'Fashion is psychology because it's about human behavior. To get on the course students have to identify some issue within the fashion industry that they believe physiology could make a positive difference towards. So it could be something that furthers knowledge, it could be something that actually campaigns for change using psychological knowledge or it could be looking at an issue that's not been investigated before. So my work here really is to produce graduates who can help make the fashion industry more ethical, more caring, more sustainable.'*
>
> Professor Carolyn Mair

A current student of Carolyn's course is a very well-known name in fashion, a woman who's been pioneering communication and championing progressive ideals within the industry since the '80s, **Caryn Franklin**, who has been referred to as a fashion oracle.

'Well, my whole space that I've been working on for a long time is body image, inclusivity and diversity. Back in the day when I started in fashion, I thought nothing of seeing middle-aged women, pensioners on the catwalk because that's what BODY MAP did and they were the coolest design duo around. They had their mums, their aunties, their clubland friends on the catwalk. If we had more of a spectrum of beauty, we would be able to see all these mixes playing out. Different body shapes, ages, ethnicities, different body types.'

Caryn Franklin @franklinonfashion

AMEN CARYN!

Ashley Graham #BeautyBeyondSize

5 tips for BODY POSITIVITY

1. Know your shape and what you feel confident in

Don't let anyone else tell you what you 'should' wear 'for your size.' It's up to you to define that. That's why thrifting is so good—it's like a giant dress-up box you can experiment with! Try things on, play, look for clothes that *you* can wear, not clothes that wear *you* and make you feel self-conscious or don't define your personality. Jump on Pinterest, check out body-positive influencers on Instagram to hunt for inspo. Start your own mood boards or keep a file of outfits you love that you can reference when thrifting.

2. Honor your shape and don't hide

No more baggy clothes and concealing. Be proud of your figure and find the bits that you feel good highlighting, whether that be a small waist, nice legs or beautiful décolletage. And don't think you can't wear jeans! Go for high-waisted, slim leg with a stretch. Show it off, sis!

An A-line shape in dresses and skirts is universally flattering.

3. Shop the men's section

You can find incredible tailoring for next to nothing, and for me personally, a lot of men's clothes just look cooler and sexier on my shape than women's clothes. They are less restrictive and really have a high-fashion vibe once styled. I steal my husband's clothes all the time.

Choose quality fabrics and more tailored cuts over quantity. It will make you look so chic and expensive for minimum spend.

4. Throw the size book out the window

Don't let a number define you. Oversized and too big are incredible to style because you can drape off the shoulder, cinch and manipulate how you want things to look. Be drawn to colors, prints, and textures you like—not a label. Try things on from all different sections of a thrift store then alter and adapt.

Don't shy away from too small necessarily either because garments that are smaller can be meshed into unison, like two large button-down shirts, for example. Try buttoning them together and wear as one. Picking contrasting colors like black and white looks especially striking. You can see this men's shirt hack on my Instagram Reels **@fayedelanty**

Cut out and replace too tight lining, crop and fray your jean cuffs to show off slim ankles, add inserts to make fitted tops more generous. If you don't know how to do this, having a tailor on speed dial is a game changer.

5. Success-ories

Accessories bring the A-game. They are an incredible way to express your personal style and elevate a look no matter your shape or size. Try brooches, statement jewelry, a great shoe or stand-out handbag. And don't forget the power of scarves! If you're having a self-conscious tummy day, try adding a scarf tucked under a belt to create a stunning asymmetrical panel over jeans or a skirt. Keep the elements fitted to show off your shape and make you feel strong.

The moral of this short story is—remove any perceived limitations and play!

You'll be amazed at what's possible.

Adaptive Clothing

The clothes we wear, the shoes we slip on, and the way we dress to greet the world say more about us than we realize. After all, fashion is a powerful art-form that allows us to own our narrative, express our individuality, and display our confidence without uttering a single word.

But not everyone shares the same thrill when they get dressed in the morning.

Currently, 15% of the world's population is experiencing some form of disability. In Australia, 20% of people have trouble dressing, finding clothes that fit, and owning their individual style. Despite this staggering figure, mainstream fashion has historically been slow to address the needs of differently-abled and elderly people.

- Buttons and zippers impede those with one-hand or limited dexterity.
- Pants and jeans are ill-fitting for people in wheelchairs and those who wear leg braces.
- Shoelaces are troublesome for those with a limb difference, and sneakers rarely accommodate leg braces.

Although adaptive clothes exist to overcome these challenges, the clothes are overly focused on function, and lack sophistication and style. Adaptive fashion revolutionizes all of that.

Adaptive fashion is specialized clothing that blends fashion and function to make getting dressed easier, pain-free, and convenient for differently-abled people. It recognizes that every one of us, irrespective of our age and body-type, has our own sense of style, so it offers trendy clothing that adapts to us. Instead of fiddly buttons, it's stylish magnetic closures that attach like magic. Instead of long shoelaces, it's one-handed zippers that make slipping on sneakers a breeze. It's jeans that are designed with a raised waist at the back and adjustable hems so they fit perfectly whether you're in a wheelchair, wearing a leg brace, or have different body proportions.

> 'The future is inclusive and we're here for it. Our products empower people to be proud of who they are–inside and out.'
>
> www.everyhuman.com.au

I have two nephews living with disabilities. Cooper, 11, is a quadriplegic after tragically receiving the incorrect treatment for Meningococcal as a baby; and Genesis, 8, was born with Cerebral Palsy. Our family friends, the Erdedis, have a Down Syndrome daughter, Simone, so I've seen first-hand the struggles these beautiful beings close to me can have with dressing and body confidence.

Thankfully for all three of them, they have incredibly dedicated parents who do everything they can to create a functional wardrobe for their kids. While it's amazing to see Tommy Adaptive and Nike jumping on board, the industry as a whole need to do more to cater for people living with disabilities. You're about to meet three amazing mums who are doing something about it.

@itsdowntosimone

Story 1: Mindy Scheier, Runway of Dreams

Excerpt from Mindy's TED talk

Life can be heartbreakingly ironic. My middle child, Oliver, was born with a rare form of muscular dystrophy. MD affects his muscle strength, his pulmonary system, distorts his body and makes every-day life more challenging than most. But my husband Greg and I told him that no matter what, he was just like everybody else. But every-day tasks for Oliver, that we all take for granted, were incredibly challenging. That simple act of dressing yourself, the very thing that I adore, was a nightmare for him. His form of MD does not affect his mind, his brain is an A+, which means he's acutely aware of his shortcomings. This became very evident when he started school, and that daily act of dressing yourself was a constant reminder of what he could and couldn't do.

So, our solution was for Oliver to wear sweatpants everyday... to school, to parties on vacations—his uniform. For special occasions he would wear proper pants but many times, because he couldn't manage the buttons and zippers... I would have to take him to the men's room, which was incredibly embarrassing for him.

For years we muddled through but when Oliver was in 3rd grade, I found out he was more like me than I ever imagined. Oliver, too, cared about fashion. He came home from school one day and said very definitively that he was going to wear jeans to school like everybody else gets to wear. Well, I certainly couldn't go to class with him and take him to the boy's room. But there was no way I was telling my eight-year-old that he couldn't wear what he wanted to wear. So that night I 'McGuyvered' the hell out of his jeans!

I remembered when I was pregnant and unwilling to stop wearing my own favorite pants—that rubber band trick. The rubber band through the buttonhole... 'round the button and back... instant stretch!

I removed the zipper so he could pull it up and down on his own. I cut up the side seam of the bottom of his pants to accommodate for his leg braces and applied Velcro. When I showed Oliver my arts and craft project he absolutely beamed. He went into school with his head held so high.

Those jeans transformed him! He was able to get dressed on his own. He was able to go to the bathroom on his own. Those jeans gave him confidence. I didn't realize it at the time but this was my first foray into adaptive clothing.

> *'When you put clothes, on you adapt the characteristics of what you're wearing whether you realize it or not. That's why you feel like a rockstar when you put on those perfect fitting jeans, that's why you feel invincible when you put on that power suit, and that's why you feel beautiful in that little black dress.'*
>
> Karen J Pine, Mind What You Wear, the Psychology of Fashion

That's exactly why Oliver felt so isolated when he couldn't wear what he wanted to wear. He even said to me one day: 'Mum, wearing sweatpants makes me feel like I'm dressing disabled.'

There are one billion people on our planet who experience some kind of disability. If 10% of that billion experience clothing challenges, that's an enormous amount of people that may not be as confident, as successful or even as happy as they could be.

> *'I realized I could do something about that and so I did! In 2013 I founded an organization called* Runway of Dreams. *The mission was to educate the fashion industry that modifications could be made to mainstream clothing for this community that has never been served.'*
>
> Mindy Scheier, Runway of Dreams

Story 2:
Juanita and Simone

These two angels pictured, are my friends—mother and daughter duo, Juanita and Simone. Simone has Down Syndrome, and when I shared Mindy's TED talk with Juanita, she really resonated with many of the getting-dressed issues she, too, faces with Simone.

FDL: Just like Mindy from Runway of Dreams, it's almost like you have to become Martha Stewart to empower your child.

JE: Yes! I wanted Simone to wear what everyone else was. I wanted her to wear jeans and to wear the uniform like everyone else. I didn't want her to wear different clothes to school because she couldn't wear the proper uniform. I did fix a lot of the clothes because when she had to go to the toilet, she couldn't do up the pants. So, I would take off the zippers, sew them up and then make them bigger, add elastic. And I always made sure she had a top over it so you wouldn't see the fixes. But honestly, she always looked beautiful. I always tried to make her look and feel beautiful, but it was bloody difficult. And more difficult as she got older. I remember her 21st, I'll never forget what this woman, a good friend of mine, said to me. Simone was wearing the most beautiful long dress, Simone looked amazing and my 'friend' said,

'Oh my god, she looks so beautiful! Everything is perfect except her shoes. Why couldn't she wear little high heels?'

And I said, 'Oh my goodness, are you kidding me? Do you honestly think that I would not let her wear them if she could!?'

Exert from full interview Chapter 13.

@itsdowntosimone

Story 3: Teata and our nephew, Genesis

'Dressing Genesis takes lots of encouragement and constant training. He definitely gets frustrated at times with how long the process can take. Because of his cerebral palsy he has to wear orthotics to help him stand and walk—they go from ankle to the knee and are very big, bulky and stiff. Made of plastic—without a barrier, the orthotics can cause irritation and sores on G's skin so he has to wear socks as protection. Problem is, socks in his size are too short so I have to buy men's but then they don't fit his feet. I have had to become a demon DIY'er, cutting, resizing, and stitching socks back up because nothing exists. The ones that do are way too expensive. I wish there was more out there, and cool stuff too—why doesn't my son deserve to have just as much swag as all the other young little dudes?'

I mean what amazing women, right?

Beautiful examples of not only the depth of a mother's love but how fashion can completely transform the way we feel.

That missing link, a perceived lack—is an opportunity for a new life, refashioned with purpose and meaning to its full expression.

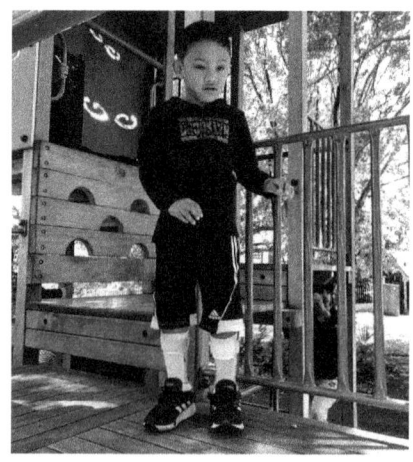

CHAPTER THREE

From Restriction to Reinvention. How I became Opshopulent

My mum and dad, London circa 1970s

The style seed for my Opshopulent awakening was unintentionally planted by my parents. From a very young age we went on weekend adventures around op shops, antique stores, vintage havens, thrift stores and garage sales as my mum, Nadia, and dad, Mick, hunted for one-of-a-kind chic.

I remember both relaying stories to me about why each piece was special. Their voices always filled with a sense of wonder; to me it was whimsical. The fact these pieces weren't new never mattered. To my parents, they were even more beautiful because they'd had a life, had time to develop their character and quirks. Everything was valued, pre-loved, had a purpose—perceived flaws and all. Honestly, I think Mum and Dad just saw their chosen shopping destinations as normal stores, no less than the departments and retail giants. There wasn't a concept of class or segregation, just all inclusive. In their generation, purchasing second hand actually gave you *proof of cool*. No matter their size, shape or color, everyone had a chance to shine. It was how they raised me to see people too.

Once home, I would marvel at Mum styling them into place, divine attention to detail. Ostrich feathers in Opshopulent vases. Art Deco lady lamps lying provocatively next to a velvet chaise lounge. Oak tables, Aubrey Beardsley mirrors, all creating a photo-shoot-worthy set which, as a poser in training, I took full advantage of!

I would raid Mum's wardrobe, create outfits and dance around in my pre-loved dream world. It made me feel so decadent! Really, let's be honest, to this day not much has changed. As a kid my nickname was Miss Piggy; if you've seen Jim Henson's *The Muppets*, it will make perfect sense why. Upon reflection, and to paraphrase mindset guru Gary Zukav, perhaps my style mothership was already showing the little fashion boat the path of my soul. A glimpse of the maiden style voyage to come[4].

Ever present were Dad's stacks of *The Face* and *British Vogue* magazines. These books became my unintentional fairy tales; I floated naturally towards them. The visuals took me somewhere so very fabulous. The character of the clothes, the language of style. Forget *Hansel and Gretel*, I wanted haute couture, honey!!

> 'How 'bout I read you a little bit of my favorite poetry… Cocktails at Tiffany's calls for classic charm. Oscar de la Renta sleeveless silk… full-skirted dress with black patent leather bow belt… Now that is pure poetry.'
>
> Carrie Bradshaw

Without realizing, these magazines became my study books, filling my head with fashion knowledge I didn't even really know I had. My Opshopulent mindset moved in by osmosis but it wasn't until years later that I meaningfully called on it.

Fashion took a detour for a while when I literally jumped out of a plane and into the most incredible job at 15 years of age. For a decade, I had the honor of being one of the hosts on Network Ten's national environmental Australian kids show, *Totally Wild*. This program was for 8-13-year-olds, but we had everyone from 8-80 watching it. Filled with fascinating facts and stories of the world around us, animals, plants, our environment… it ran for 30 years! It finally shut up shop in 2021.

I used to sit at home watching the program wishing I was on there, then after a stint of work experience and a hint of destiny via a tandem sky dive for a story on the show, it became a reality. I travelled the country reporting on everything from ants to aeronautical engineers, lemurs to legless lizards, carnivorous plants to recycling furniture. *Totally Wild* not only taught me the full spectrum of storytelling—researching, writing, producing, presenting and even editing—it forever connected me to our planet and my purpose to protect her.

No job you have is a mistake. I believe it leads you to your divine calling, as did *Totally Wild*. I learnt patience, how to find common ground with all walks of life, and the ability to adapt and think on my feet. Let me tell you, working with kids and animals—aka pure spirits with the only agenda to be themselves—was a daily b-lesson (blessing and a lesson!). However, even being on the show for 10 years, all my colleagues still saw me as the fashion girl. In fact, the make-believe animal genus they created for me was the I-Like-To-Shop-a-Lot-us (which is now the I-like-to-OP-SHOP-a-lot-us, I guess!).

Style was in my bones and it was trying to find a way out. Sadly, it expressed itself in the excessive way for most of my twenties. I think I may have partly funded the success of iconic Australian brand sass & bide. More is more was definitely my muse. If you'd told me back then that a decade later, I would become an eco-stylist, I would have asked you what that was!? While environmentalism was my daily bread, it hadn't broken into my consciousness fully yet.

After a decade of animal storytelling, the fashion wild was still calling. It was time to finally answer. I leapt again into the unknown and head-first into nothingness, never imagining it would lead me to my second dream job. In fact it was really difficult for quite a few years. I felt lost, unsure of my next step and afraid to take it but everything I was looking for was right under my nose. It just took me some time to sniff it out.

Returning to the motherland in 2012 was a complete re-awakening for me. Time in my British birth place, Surrey at 'Magical Aunty Land'—aka my Aunty Zena's place—was seriously so wonderful, as were our charity shop challenges, but more on that later!

My virgin sighting of serious snow inspired me to create my very first blog post, 'Everything goes with snow', showcasing the insanely cool vintage jackets my dad gave me from his collection.

He had these incredible pieces made bespoke in London in the '70s by the same tailor, Tommy Nutter, who handcrafted garments for The Beatles, Led Zeppelin, The Rolling Stones and Elton John. These jackets are absolute showstoppers and the story behind them is sublime; they were definitely the catalyst for my Opshopulent journey.

Living in London and NYC on a tight travel budget and no job, forced me to slow down, spend less and restyle the way I was doing things. A forced fashion detox was just what the doctor ordered and so my unintentional pre-loved PhD began. My childhood past-time became my practical adult reality. I see now what an absolute blessing that was.

BIBLE STUDY

British Vogue quickly became my bible, schooling me again on every aspect of the fashion world. The editorials taught me styling, structure, attention to detail, creativity. The curve of a bow and how a cuff could be just so. The advertorials were my brand DNA analysis work. I came to understand what Chanel and Louis Vuitton looked like, the form of Fendi, how Dior draped. Almost architecturally crafted articles kept me across trends, history, designers, popular culture and opinion pieces igniting the fashion storyteller in me.

> 'When I first moved to NYC,
> I would buy *Vogue* instead of food,
> I just felt it fed me more.'
> Carrie Bradshaw

All this intel would equip me on my eco-shopping trips. I couldn't afford Chanel but why couldn't I create the feel!?

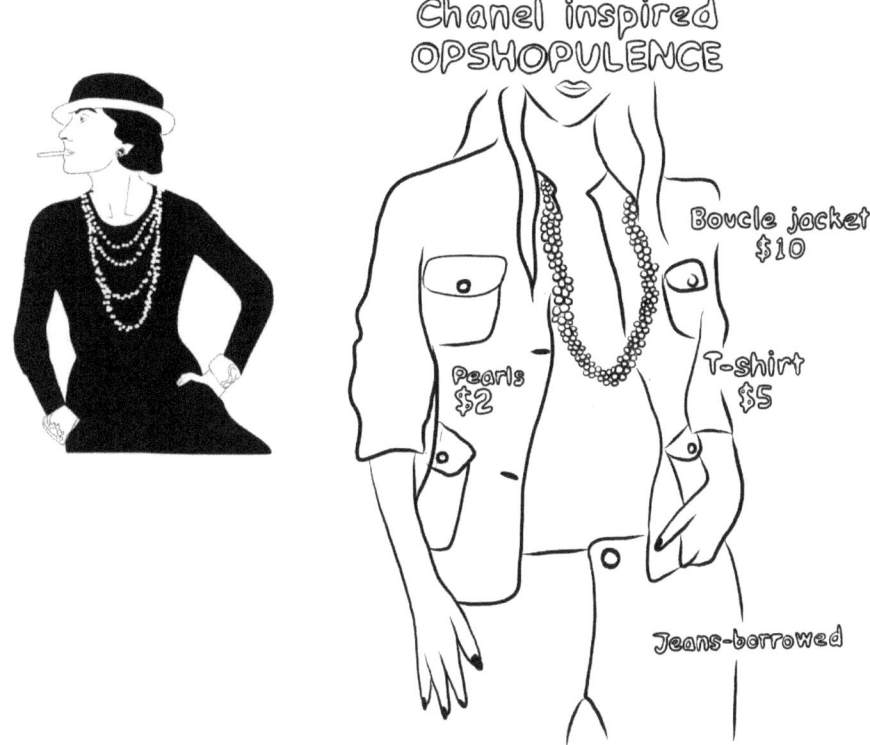

> 'In order to be irreplacable one
> must always be different.'
>
> Coco Chanel

With a minimal allowance, I would head to my local thrift store to dream up all manner of ways to get luxe for less and it wasn't long before people noticed. I remember a particular London evening, my best friend Karen and I were heading to a very well-to-do party in Notting Hill, and Karen was sporting some serious designer. I decided to rock a $5 band tee and a $10 vintage black velvet fascinator hat with skinny leg jeans and heels, because well, that's what I had and I had to make it work. But you know what? It really did work!

Throughout the evening people kept complimenting me on my unique outfit and asking where I got it. At first, I was shy to reveal the story but my sweet best friend proudly told all the socialites that I'd got the look from a charity store for under 20 quid. Somehow, among a sea of labels I had become the luxe standout. Necessity and restriction really was my mother of all re-invention!

That simple act of a supportive best friend, single-handedly gave me the confidence to show off my Opshopulence.

Settling back into Australia, a TV opportunity sparked the idea to connect with the charity retail sector, never imagining it would lead me to my dream job. Freddy Choo, I am forever grateful to you. Thank you for seeing me.

A passage in Deepak Chopra's book *The 7 Spiritual Laws of Success* propelled me even further:

> 'I will ask myself daily,
> "How can I serve?"
> and "How can I help?"'
>
> Deepak Chopra, Excerpt below from *The 7 Spiritual Laws of Success*

> ## The Law of Dharma or Purpose in Life
>
> *Everyone has a purpose in life, a unique gift or special talent to give to others. And when we blend this unique talent with service to others, we experience the ecstasy and exultation of our own spirit, which is the ultimate goal.*
>
> *I will put the Law of Dharma into effect by making a commitment to take the following steps:*
>
> 1. *Today I will lovingly nurture the god or goddess in embryo that lies deep within my soul. I will pay attention to the spirit within me that animates both my body and my mind. I will awaken myself to this deep stillness within my heart. I will carry the consciousness of timeless, eternal Being in the midst of time-bound experience.*
>
> 2. *I will make a list of my unique talents. Then I will list all the things that I love to do while expressing my unique talents. When I express my unique talents and use them in the service of humanity, I lose track of time and create abundance in my life as well as in the lives of others.*
>
> 3. *I will ask myself daily, "How can I serve?" and "How can I help?" The answers to these questions will allow me to help and serve my fellow human beings with love.*

That sentence lit my soul on fire. It completely covered me in goosebumps, and you know what?

Goosebumps *never lie.*

It was my '*aha moment,*' as Oprah calls it. Through using my unique gifts I could see how I could help a charity bring more funds to their mission, make op shopping chic, and allow me to follow my calling to be of service through style.

In the beginning, a lot of people thought I was a little nuts or that 'quirky hippy girl who wore hemp' (yep, seriously!), but I really feel now it was divinely guided because I dared to follow my bliss. Years ago, in my searching phase, a friend asked me, 'What do you do when you're "wasting time"!?' Such a potent question. I discovered under the layers of perceived procrastination, I actually found my good fortune and most fulfilling way forward.

'What did you do as a child that created timelessness, that made you forget time? There lies the myth to live in.'

Joseph Campbell

You see when I was happy, I would thrift. If I was sad, I would thrift. No matter how I felt, I would always thrift, and it's the same with magazines. I used to feel a sense of guilt for the giant stack of magazines that lined the corners of my bedroom but then my dad said the coolest thing, 'Don't worry, kiddo, one day these books will pay you back,' and he was right in more ways than one.

Enter Salvos Stores

The Salvation Army is a super brand, a global charity focused on being of service and empowering the community. Founded in England by William Booth, they have an incredible mission and work tirelessly to assist local community members who are going through some challenging stuff. We're talking drug and alcohol addiction, domestic violence, gambling issues, depression, loss of confidence, and homelessness. Their retail op shops in Australia known as 'Salvos Stores' form the backbone of the charity with 100% of the profits going straight back into the mission of the Salvation Army.

'As National Director, my responsibility is to ensure that Salvos Stores plays its part in sustaining the Salvation Army's mission of giving hope where it's needed most well into the future. In a practical sense this means I get to lead a team of incredibly passionate people in enabling literally millions of Australians to make a social and environmental impact.'

Matt Davis, Salvos Stores CEO

1,000,000+ SESSIONS OF CARE
10,000 VOLUNTEERS
$36 MILLION RAISED
350+ STORES
(as of 2021)

Salvos Stores are stocked by using second hand public donations: the main portion is clothing but there is also plenty of furniture, homewares, haberdashery, electrical, books and toys to be found. Not only are these pre-loved portals a one-stop shop but they are also, by nature, one of the largest urban recyclers, diverting hundreds of thousands of textile waste from landfill every year.

'Fashion and textiles have always been a huge part of the op shop experience. Representing about half of all the items we sell. Salvos Stores diverts about 20,000 tonnes every year.'

Matt Davis, Salvos Stores CEO

When I started my journey with sustainability and thrifting, I definitely saw a perceived stigma. 'Op shopping isn't cool,' that's for 'poor people,' 'it's a great place to find a costume or something retro.' I was determined to shift this way of thinking, and I've stuck to it because I truly believe it's BS! To me, thrifting just makes perfect economic, environmental, and planet/people-friendly sense, especially when you discover it never, ever has to mean sacrificing style, and the incredible support it can bring to members of the community.

> *'When I was in Adelaide a couple of years ago, I met a mother who spends a day each week sitting on the lounges in our furniture section. Our store manager explained to me that her 30-year-old son had an acquired brain injury from a motor vehicle accident and that he only remembers his father, not his mother. So that her son didn't become distressed during their visits to the care facility each week, her husband would drop her at the store for the day. While devastating, she felt safe and welcome by our team. It was a very special moment for me to understand the many ways lives can be transformed. It is my hope that these examples of human connection, one life at a time, always remain true for us.'*
>
> Matt Davis, Salvos Stores CEO

This beautiful memory from Matt is exactly why I do what I do. This is the power these bricks and mortars can have. To be a beacon of light in a dark time, to welcome one and all, I mean it's just the easiest decision of where I want to spend my money and to use my skills to be of service for this unbelievably important cause. My way is via our wardrobes—I feel like this is a place we are all open to communicating through.

Op shopping and recreating high-end chic with second hand clothing makes me incredibly happy, and I am so proud to be the eco-stylist and media ambassador for Salvos Stores Australia, eight years and counting.

It's incredible how much has shifted in the last eight years. Thrifting is now totally relevant, in fact it's become the height of fashion-forward thinking. Now is the perfect time to share my message of Opshopulence!

Artist's impression of models from one of my thrift-chic TV segments

My role with Salvos Stores is many and varied. Merging from eco-styling, to talking on the tele, to exchanging wisdom with staff, creating initiatives like our Salvos Street Boutiques, Morning TV segments to runway shows and eco-events. All aimed at elevating and innovating the face of second hand fashion retail. Basically, it's my job to show consumers why op shopping is so insanely cool, and a powerful way to vote with your fashion dollar.

The Salvos Street Boutiques

The Australian Salvos Street boutiques are an idea Salvos and I developed to help the stores elevate their stock, appeal to a wider demographic, and increase funds for the mission of the Salvation Army. A mini-store within a store aimed at taking the guess work out of thrifting and creating a higher-end boutique shopping experience yet one that remains at op shop prices!

All clothing in these sections is curated, color-coded and styled; they are all from public donations. You will find current trends, shop-able capsule collections, outfit suggestions, wooden hangers, and space to see the clothes, creating a more seamless way to thrift. It's perfect for the time-poor, thrifting rookies who regularly walk away due to op shopping overwhelm, seasoned professionals seeking a more stylized shopping experience and especially for the not yet converted! The Salvos Street Boutiques look like a high-street store; however, instead of a fast-fashion fix they offer a slow

and sustainable experience which not only elevates your look but gives a serious leg-up to local community. But don't worry if you love the thrill of the kill, you can still head into the grass roots of the rest of the store and really get thrifty with it. These sections are designed as a complement and never to compete—you can have a scout around the boutique and grab an on-trend bargain then team it with a fun find from the clearance rack. It's all about op-tions, people!

Salvos and I started with one boutique and now we have 32 across most Australian states. Collectively, and to date, they have made well over a million dollars, and 100% of that goes straight back into the mission of the Salvation Army. We now also have our first By Appointment Bridal Boutique in Wollongong, NSW, which was launched exclusively on the *Today Show* no less. The boutique concept continues to grow and evolve.

Let's be honest, we humans are visual creatures and for the most part no matter how sustainable something is, if it doesn't make us look and feel cool, we won't buy into it. Add to this, the word 'eco,' which can quite often conjure images of hemp, unkept hippies, and no connection to chic. That's why I knew the boutiques would work because if you make it 'cute,' they will come.

'A big opportunity that I know you are passionate about, Faye, is bringing things that may seem exclusive, within reach. For many customers seeking a high-end experience, op shops may seem unable to fit the bill. I believe that through the advocacy of key influencers, learning how to pull a great outfit together and op shops continuing to improve how they curate on-trend items, we can continue to help Australians see new possibilities.'

Matt Davis, Salvos Stores CEO

Head to www.salvosstores.com.au to find a boutique near you and to learn more about the amazing work of the Salvation Army.

DID YOU KNOW?

Here's a fascinating little ditty on the origins of where the Australian term for thrifting—op shopping—came from, as beautifully crafted by Robyn Anneal in her book *Nothing New: A history of second hand*.

Millie Tallis came up with the idea. It was the winter of 1925 and St. Vincent's Hospital was looking to expand. A fundraising appeal was launched, headed by Melbourne's Lord Mayor and a committee of worthies that included Sir George Tallis. Sir George had made his fortune as a theatrical impresario and his good lady wife—before she was wife, of course—had starred, in tights and satin bloomers, as a comic-opera 'gem.' Now the pair shone bright in the constellation of Melbourne Society. Over the course of several months, raffles were held and balls mounted, there was a car rally, a beauty contest, a telephone girls' carnival, a brass and extravaganza—the usual things. Also usual would have been a jumble sale held over one to two days in a hall with room enough for trestle tables and the serving of tea.

But the St. Vincent's committee had at its disposal something better than just any old hall: on the site of the hospital's proposed expansion stood the Cyclorama. Forty meters in diameter, with a high-domed roof, the

Cyclorama was built in 1889 to house a 360-degree painted panorama that audiences viewed from a central platform. Lady Tallis and her husband had just returned from a motoring tour that took them through France and across the U.S., where they'd witnessed the popularity of second hand shops run on charitable lines. Why not try something similar in aid of St. Vincent's? A shop, rather than a jumble sale? Lady Tallis took charge and in christening the enterprise paid a nod to its continental progenitor, *le magazine d'occasion*. But while the French occasion here signifies 'bargain' it can also be used to mean 'opportunity'. Did Lady Tallis mistranslate? Or, was it a knowing distinction she made, or even a small cross-lingual pun? Whichever it was, it came to pass that, for three months straddling Christmas 1925, the Cyclorama played host to the first ever 'opportunity shop.'

NOW LET US MUSE ON THE FOUNDATIONAL MANTRA OF AN OPSHOPULENT MINDSET...

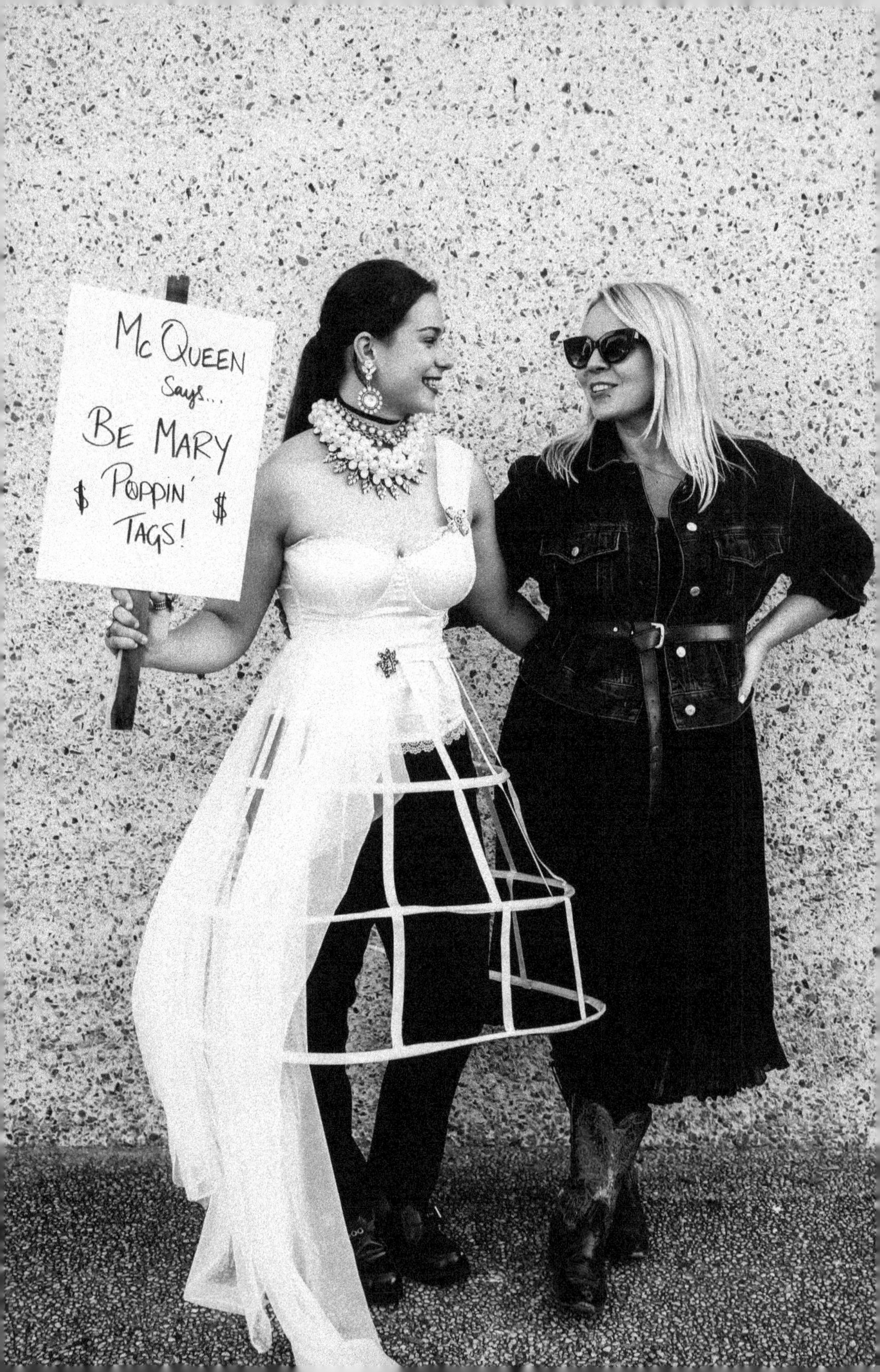
Mc QUEEN
says...
BE MARY
$ POPPIN' $
TAGS!

CHAPTER FOUR

The ABC of Opshopulence

> 'Abundance is not something we acquire. It's something we become.'
>
> Wayne Dyer

Opshopulence is a state of mind and it's really only a shift in thought and a sustainably styled outfit away. It's as simple as learning your ABCs. This is an easy-to-follow foundational Mantra for Opshopulence, which will help you align with your action steps:

A–bundance mindset
B–elieve in the underdog
C–are for the planet

ABUNDANCE MINDSET

Cast your mind back to my opening story and the girl (aka me) who I described absolutely slaying it in the outfit stakes. She looked a million bucks but only spent $50. Now that is excessive amounts of sass!

Giving off an air of expensive has nothing to do with a big bank account or the label on a jacket, it's all about your attitude. How you hold yourself, the way you walk into a room, your ability to inspire and make others feel good. The cool little splashes of signature style you weave into your outfit—now *that* drips of abundance to me.

When it comes to dressing yourself deluxe it's all about preparation meeting opshop-portunity!

As we now know, my mum didn't grow up with much, so she found a way to see the beauty in even the most inexpensive of things. From this evolved approach, she developed an incredible knack of making the forgotten so insanely fabulous.

She inadvertently taught me to do the same.

Removing judgment of where these clothes came from or how they are perceived and instead focusing on the incredible change they have the power to evoke, opens the door to a decadent way to dress. Great style is never about how much you spend, it's all about perception. I see the possibility in pre-loved clothing and it gives me great pleasure to bend, twist and re-style once-discarded items into a new dimension.

'The power of pretty,' as I like to call it.

I've seen it to full effect with our Salvos Street Boutiques.

> 'In the world of marketing it doesn't matter what you think; unless we make this sexy to a whole new generation it ain't gonna happen.'
>
> Mary Portas, in conversation with Bay Garret on her podcast *This Old Thing!*

Florence @stylebyflossy and Munya @munyabrown1 in my Thrift shop ode to Versace

Instead of feeling 'restricted', use the challenge to create a complete reinvention.

Instead of a fast-fashion haul, *overhaul your mind and the way you see second hand.*

Once you start, you'll be so excited by what's possible with pre-loved clothing. To me, true abundance is in giving to yourself, others and our gorgeous planet. Inspiring your fellow human friends to invest in a different way of thinking is a divine form of abundance; to see a light bulb go off for someone or to ignite a change in lifestyle choices is something money will never be able to buy.

Change your fashion mindset, change your wardrobe life for GOOD!

Scarcity Fashion Mindset People

These are the ones who are holding on for dear life:

'I've got to have more clothes.'

'I might never get another opportunity for that item.'

Everything is *more more more* because they worry about having *less less less*.

Abundance Fashion Mindset People

These are the ones who are ok with letting go.

If something comes their way and it doesn't work or they missed a sale, it's not a worry for they believe there is a whole world of opportunity out there.

If you have an abundance mindset you're naturally fine with:

Fashion FOMO (fear of missing out)

Happy going with the flow and having less

Abundance fashion mindset people are centered around the idea that you don't need stuff, and that the things you do buy make a sustainable difference.

Musings by @mrpatrickduffy

BELIEVE IN
THE UNDERDOG

'One never knows what joy one might find among the unwanted and abandoned.'

Lola, *Kinky Boots*

There is unlimited opportunity in a thrift store; it's just up to you to uncover it. I find this so incredibly exciting and much prefer the creative autonomy it inspires over having it all fed to me by the mass market. Seriously, set yourself an excursion and go into a high-street store on a busy day and observe the goings on—the pumping music, bright lights of 'buy me now', the long change room lines, stacks of wear-once style draped over customers' arms, a sort of blank stare and a searching for fashion fulfilment.

Most importantly, commit to not buying a thing and challenge yourself to consider how much of what they have might already be in your wardrobe or could be found among the racks of second hand fashion stores. I don't say this to be judgmental of the experience but more to bring awareness of how we can all get whipped into a wardrobe frenzy. Then try visiting a thrift store or a slow-fashion boutique and see the parallels.

There's a small little street near where I live in Sydney that is an absolute favorite of mine. On William Street, all the boutiques are independently owned, work off the smaller run model, have a slow production ethos and the loveliest part is the conversations that ensue. You get to meet the maker and connect to their story, which of course becomes your story. My friend Emily has a store here, it's actually Australia's first zero-waste designer rental boutique and she does absolutely all of it herself from sourcing to selling and is so passionate about the pre-loved industry.

> 'Driven by an authentic commitment to
> social justice and environmental responsibility,
> we aim to change people's perception that
> luxury has to mean "new".'
>
> Emily Kate Symes, EKOLUV Founder @ekoluv

You'll get to meet Emily towards the end of this book in my Opshopulence interview series. Plus, you'll see Emily modeling along with other incredible members of my Opshopulent community. They each have a great story to tell, and I can't wait for you to see them shine and feel inspired by their missions.

Second hand allows you to reconnect to what you wear and why you're wearing it, which in turn is a wonderful way to develop your own personal style quirks. Make like Lola and be a champion for the cast aside. Trust me, there is a ton of happiness that awaits you.

Care For The Planet

I mean really is there any other way to be? We've done a staggering job of stuffing up the Earth so now we really owe it to the Mother to do what we can to create change.

Don't worry about trying to fix everything in one go. Just begin where you are, with simple switches. I promise you, individual impact is powerful beyond what you realize and has a profound ripple effect. So, start small and by shopping consciously, head into your local op shop or small business and choose eco-chic over high-street sheep.

Be the light for those around you but never preach. Instead allow them to ask questions when they're ready. Once you're rocking Opshopulence, they will definitely be trying to find out more.

It's not about age, demographic or denomination, Opshopulence has everything to do with a shift in perception and creating a movement by rewiring our mindset. Fashion is an incredibly powerful platform, so why wouldn't we use it to be a force for good?

Some really poignant questions to ask yourself are:

- What kind of fashion future do I want to vote for?
- How could I be of service through my style choices?
- Does my wardrobe currently empower the world around me?
- Is it empowering me?

The way I see it, our closets can be an incredible catalyst for change, and to me that is Opshopulence to the core.

As you gather momentum, keep the 'ABC' front of mind; it will serve as a mission statement you can return to whenever you feel off course.

And remember... progress over perfection!

My thrift-styled models, Revive Festival, Brisbane 2019

CHAPTER FIVE

Developing your Signature Opshopulent Style

I truly believe op-shopping has been the catalyst for the clarity I have around my personal style. It has allowed me to play and explore all manner of possibilities. My perceived restriction has been my absolute reinvention. I've found that defining my signature style has helped me significantly reduce the dreaded *I have nothing to wears*, built my confidence, and truly impacted how I interact, hold myself and communicate with the world around me. What a beautiful journey it has been and now it brings me great joy to pass the wisdom on to you.

Dive into this exercise below.

Ask yourself all the juicy questions, grab a notebook and pen, get busy and you'll be expressing your own signature Opshopulent style in no time.

1. Define your lifestyle

What does your day-to-day require of you?

For me, every day is different. I could be in among thrift clothes sourcing for a shoot, helping to set up a new boutique, speaking to the media, perched in front of my laptop, creating content or visiting stores.

While I absolutely love beautiful things and big heels, that's really not going to sustain me with what my work demands. Don't think for a second that *cute* has to be escorted from the building.

I've slowly developed a sneaky style system that ensures functionality can absolutely form a long-lasting friendship with fashion.

I like to call it *beaut-ility*.

2. Who or what inspires you?

Take the time to think about who or what fires you up in terms of fashion and style.

Here is a snapshot of some of the things that inspire me:

- Street Style—how a girl can rock a super simple dress but she carries herself like a Queen. A guy who has gone all out in a hat, spats and cravat.
- New York City and London—the places, the people, the sub-cultures, the style diversity.
- Music and music icons—I love Robert Plant, Keith Richards and 'It' girls like Anita Pallenberg, Brigitte Bardot and Kate Moss. That 'dirty pretty' kinda feel.
- Art Deco—the divinely decadent design era from the 1920's and 30's. As an easy point of reference think *The Great Gatsby*.
- 1950s DIOR—the incredibly technical artistry. The way everything draped and dipped just so. Did you know Dior wanted to be an architect before he chose fashion design! .
- Bespoke tailoring—Garment construction made by hand and from scratch based on a customer's specifications. Bespoke tailoring offers Incredible attention to detail, thought and skill set. Many of the true bespoke tailoring greats herald from Savile Row, London.
- Vintage jewelry—The detail, considered production and of course the shiny sparkles, so much story in bling from bygone days.
- Outfit attention to detail and dichotomy—think sequins with army fatigues, distressed denim with lace, cowboy boots with pretty pleats.
- Brooches and belts—both for me, bring such a beautiful finish to an outfit. I especially love vintage offerings.
- Classic timeless simplicity—a crisp white button down with faded vintage levi's. A silk slip dress and tailored blazer...fashion poetry!

What are your inspirations?

Write them down, do some image searching and ignite that creative fashion fire.

Get clear on what resonates with you. It's ok if it isn't clear straight away, keep musing and exploring. Try it all; the answers will arrive.

@shopportunityvintage upcycled necklace

3. Envision your ideal style and come up with three words to describe it

This will become your signature Opshopulent style mantra.

To give you an example, mine is:

TIMELESS, TAILORED, QUIRK

It became clear to me after doing a little mind map of words and elements, that what I love in outfits and why they resonate with me is that I appreciate tailoring, crave functionality, yet I like to be different.

I also asked a few friends who know me well for their thoughts.

So now I invite you to mind map...

Faye De Lanty
@fayedelanty

Giving off an air of expensive has nothing to do with a big bank account or the label on a jacket. It's all about your attitude. How you hold yourself, the way you walk into a room, your ability to make others feel good. Clothes that spark change. That's true abundance to me.

12:01pm 31/1/21 Twitter

Finding Your 'Style Dosha'

In Ayurvedic culture, Doshas are the three energies that define every person's make up. Knowing your Dosha can help you live a healthier, more balanced life (**chopra.com**).

As a starting point, muse on these words and circle in pencil or write down in your notebook the ones which resonate most:

> Classic, cool, French, functional, timeless, elegant, playful, colorful, considered, earthy, sharp, bold, modern, minimalistic, mindful, retrospective, neutral, bright, old Hollywood, tribal, rock, preppy, pretty, new/romantic, strong, sexy, curvy, monochromatic, metallic, rainbow, chameleon, European, Stockholm/Scando, New York, Bohemian, Brit, East London, Punk, deconstructed, converted, one-of-a-kind, pin-up, rustic, regal, business, androgynous, non-binary, dandy, femme, masculine, fresh, crisp, clean, cultivated, chaos, clash, cut well, diaphanous, steampunk, rockabilly, soft, eclectic, vintage, diaphanous, Mori Kei (natural fabrics/nature theme), relaxed, surfer-chic, Hamptons, happy, couture-ified.

Now write some of your own words that come to mind.

Your three words could become clear quite quickly or it may be something you muse on over a few weeks or more. There is no time limit. Remember, this is slow-fashion, my friends. Take your time and get to know your 'style you.' Keep musing, be kind, the words will show up. Once you discover your style dosha (or three words), I would love for you to share it with me on Instagram **@fayedelanty** and show me a 'new to you' (second hand) look honoring your style dosha or archetype.

4. That's so PIN-TERESTING!

Create a mood-board, put together a collage, collate an album on your phone or collect magazine tears. Whatever works best for you, keep it all in the one spot so its cohesive and easy to reference. You can also create sub-categories on Pinterest like rock tees or little black dresses or statement coats.

Join me on Pinterest **@fashionhound**

I've made some special Opshopulence boards for you to be inspired by.

5. What is your signature? What is it about you that stands out or that people know you for?

For moi?

People know me for my brooches, and other elements such as scarves, a cinched waist, sharp jackets and a full skirt. I wear a lot of neutrals—black, white, caramel or leopard print (that's totally a neutral if you ask me) but I'll give them quirk by choosing to wear a stand-out like:

- Vintage lace up leather boots
- A serious brooch stack
- Corsetry
- A tailored or bespoke jacket

I really believe in the power of bringing your accessories A-game. Simple classic pieces step it up to the next level with a considered placement of pretty. If this feels like an overwhelming question, for now just start by thinking about the things you really love and what you'd feel fabulous yet functional wearing. Write down some buzz words, ask your friends, check out street style and start to gather intel on what you are gravitating towards.

6. Do a closet edit

Pull out the pieces that fit with your personal style dosha (your three words) and be honest about what fits into your ideal look.

As we know, my style dosha is: Timeless, Tailored, Quirk.

So think:

- A beautifully tailored suit
- Pleated midi skirts
- White tee, in fact ALL the butter-soft tee incarnations including rock and vintage to fulfil my QUIRK brief
- High-waisted pants
- Effortless summer dresses in natural fibers and neutral tones
- Silk scarves, scarves and more scarves
- Statement, well-made shoes
- Stripes
- Stand out one-of-a-kind bags
- BLINGGGGGGG because... *brooches*

I also have a small collection of one-of-a-kind vintage dresses because they have the most divine unique qualities and really stand out from the crowd. I aim to be picky here too, leaning more towards velvet, silk, rayon and taffeta because they are a breeze to wear but still really bold and unique.

Crazy prints, ill-fitting form and fabric, restrictive cuts and copious amounts of color be gone!

I get my kicks from contrast, detail, and accessories definition teamed with the classic side of town.

This is me.

Do the same for *you* and be honest with what truly sits within your ideal situation—sell, share, or donate the rest.

7. Define what's missing and make a list

I'm still looking for:

- A white, timeless summer dress
- A classic black leather carry-all bag
- The perfect white and black silk slip
- The ultimate pair of vintage Levis
- and let's be honest, there's always room for more brooches

I look to thrift my items first but if I can't, I keep an eye on Etsy, Gumtree and local smaller brands and boutiques. I'm happy to wait so I can stay true to my values, and really, there is something so Opshopulent about a lust-list and the longing. Wherever you go, be discerning about what you allow into your wardrobe and make sure it continues to tick all the boxes of your three-word brief.

8. Go thrifting

Check out the charity shop challenge in Chapter 10 for some great inspiration and ideas. Take your list and your reference pictures with you or refer to your Pinterest boards so you don't get off track and topple into a shop-fest.

Do leave room for surprise on your treasure hunt though! Thrifting can be so amazingly unexpected.

9. Play dress-ups

Seriously, who doesn't love a fashion show in their own lounge room!? Explore what you have, take some time to put together outfit ideas and try different combinations. Connect with your inner child. Make a note of it or even better, snap some pics so you have a reference point to go back to when you're not sure what to wear. You'll be so surprised what's possible by shopping your own wardrobe!

Stay tuned for the **#wardrobeworkout** in Chapter 9

10. Don't be afraid to replicate

It's ok to recreate a look you love from head to toe until you get your confidence up. Your signature will put an original stamp on it anyway. If I really like something, I emulate what I see but just with a Faye kind of flavor.

Some of my beloved brooches pinned on a bustier.

NOW IT IS TIME FOR

THE HOW TO

100+
Ideas to Unlock Your Opshopulence

This is the section to put your Opshopulence into practice. Among these pages are an abundance of ideas for restyling, elevating, and getting your professional thriftanista on. These are my tried and tested methods that never let me down, and I know they will do the same for you.

These ideas are quick, easy, and elegant techniques to totally transform your thrift finds into the next style dimension.

Behold 100-plus ideas to unlock your Opshopulence, modeled by members of my Opshopulent and thrifty community from all parts of the globe.

Different ages, sizes, ethnicities, expressions and all incredibly eco-chic. I can't wait for you to meet them.

CHAPTER SIX

Op Shop decoder —overwhelm BE GONE

Crazy amounts of clothes and color, over-stacked, back-breaking racks to sift through, a sea of shoes and accessories. Don't worry, I completely understand your overwhelm. It's one of the biggest pieces of feedback I receive about thrift shopping—that it's just too much and it's impossible to know where to start.

Even if you do have a desire to create a more conscious wardrobe, the state of some thrift stores can put you off and steer you away from exploring, I get it. Especially when it doesn't look like there would be anything cute in there but trust me there totally is! In fact, it's a glam goldmine.

That was one of the big reasons I created the Street Boutique concept with the Salvos: to take the guesswork out of getting thrifty with it and offer a more streamlined experience. You can absolutely do that for yourself too. I have spent my life in these havens and developed a fine art of not only refashioning thrift but being able to break them down fast. As with any new undertaking its always best to start simply, slowly, and build your confidence one fabulous find at a time.

CONSIDER MY TOP 10 TIPS AS YOU EMBARK ON YOUR THRIFT-VENTURE...

(These can help you with online thrifting too!)

1. Educate Yourself

Knowledge is power. The more you know, the more you will be able to really fine-tune the thrifting experience. All those years spent exploring *British Vogue* have really paid off for me because now I know how to *Fendi-ify* or style a *Salvation Ar-mani* silhouette.

The editorials in these magazines are a great muse of course but there is just as much wisdom to uncover by exploring the advertorials. By that I mean all the high-end designer ads you see at the beginning of a fashion publication like *Vogue*. Sure they pay for the publication to stay in circulation, but believe me, they will fund your eco-fashion journey too. Study the clothes, signature accents, color palette and the way the outfits are put together. Make note of the features of the collection, the hardware intrinsic to this brand—logos, trims and signature colors like Tiffany blue or Hermès orange. This is all part of their signature and the message they are trying to share.

Let us consider Chanel for a moment.

This iconic French design house is famous for its boucle jackets, chain strap bags, pearls and pretty camellia brooches. Every season they take those staples for a style journey focusing on a particular country, time, color palette or a message from popular culture. The fundamentals of what make up Chanel, however, remain the same. So when you are thrifting, hunt for items that have a similar Chanel aesthetic and you'll be able to create a cool op shop ode without having to spend copious amounts of cash.

Try a simple thrifted white tee and jeans with a tweed/boucle jacket and chain strap bag and drape a string of pearls for added appeal. This is Opshopulence in action!

Another absolutely endless inspiration portal for me is the Vogue Runway app. It has every high-end designer and includes *all* their collections, reviews on the brands, plus street style from every fashion week that occurs throughout the year. This is where I stay abreast of what's big every season, to help me create looks for myself but also for our stores, our community and any special events I am producing.

This also subconsciously builds an intel inside my fashion brain, where certain thrifted garments will generate an idea or spark a concept I know I can recreate. As my bikram yoga teacher Katie says on consistency with practice: 'It's money in the bank, babe.'

Visiting high-street and high-end stores regularly will also add deposits to your style account. The more you immerse yourself, the more creative and quick witted you will become.

2. Be Prepared

While it's fun to be a fashion free spirit, and I think it's extremely exhilarating to stay open to the surprise nature of thrifting, I must say there's been definite merit in getting my girl scout on and being prepared. I keep an open mind to the chance of something magical and unexpected popping up; however, I find that having my eye on the prize massively reduces my op shop overwhelm. Take a list, photo inspiration and get really picky about what is *added to cart*. Such a philosophy will prevent you from time wasting, grabbing whatever catches your attention, feeling flustered, decision fatigue, and ultimately buying a bunch of stuff you don't really need.

Say you have a black tuxedo jacket and a simple white tee on your thrifty lust-list, then do yourself a favor and get really one-pointed about searching only for those things. Be picky too. Hold the garment up to the light, check for marks, flaws and faults, examine the fabric quality. Is it well made? Does it fit you like a glove (or if it's a designer find, could you have it altered?). Will you love and wear this time and again? Does it fit into your day-to-day and style mantra? Is it comfortable?

When you nail this, it will build your confidence, and next time you go looking for a few things on your thrift list—while again staying open to what might pop up—slowly, slowly you will catch your style monkey.

P.S. Be sure to **dress for it**.

Wear something that's really easy to change in and out of or try fitted clothing that allows you to try things on over the top. Think leggings, loose jeans or a simple slip off/under dress. Honestly, there's nothing more annoying than having to take a thousand things off.

Chanel-inspired jacket $10, pearls $2, tee $5 all thrifted @salvosstores

3. Follow The Fashion Fundamentals
—All hail the anti-trends

Seek out and stick to the classics. These are what I like to call *canvas pieces*, and whether you're a princess or a punk they will serve you well. Think denim, leather biker jackets, great belts, t-shirts and trench coats, for example. These items form the beginning of a bangin' outfit. Start here and then you can add your style mantra to make it intrinsically you, even if you're of the mohawk persuasion!

My **30 things to thrift** in the next chapter will set you on your way.

Op shops are filled with great versions of these timeless, *anti-trend* or trendless pieces and once you have them you can build and play with personality from there. Practice discernment. Pick canvas pieces that even though they might be pre-loved, are in pristine condition. You want these items to go the distance and be wearable season after season.

Opshopulence isn't just about grabbing a bargain, it's about being really mindful that the clothes we invite into our life not only support the planet, but also serve us in their sustainability. Less and really measured will give you such a feeling of luxe. Focus on fabrics, form and fabulous detail like bold buttons, double stitching and serious beaut-ility (wearable, functional beauty).

4. Throw The Size Book Out The Window

And the labels too. This is one of the key elements as to why I adore thrifting; you don't have to answer to or be intimidated by a number or a name. I have thrifted items in my wardrobe that range from a size 8 to a size 18+ and they all fit beautifully for different reasons. I have learnt to try everything on and practice non-judgment, choosing freedom over fashion restriction.

While it's nice to discover a designer item, I've found:

- $25 Manolo Blahniks with the $850 price tag still on the sole
- $30 vintage Yves Saint Laurent men's wool blazer with beautiful, monogrammed buttons
- $1 silk Hermès scarf
- $2 Moschino belt

To name but a few.

These are some of the designer pieces I have uncovered thrifting over the years. Yes, sure it's amazing to find pre-loved high-end like this, however I can get just as excited about a no-name vintage or inexpensive garment. If it speaks to me, it speaks to me. Just because something is 'high-end' doesn't mean it's automatically chic.

Opshopulence has rewarded me with a renewed sense of self and closet inclusivity.

It's far more important for me now to be one-of-a-kind than one of the sizing masses.

Pre-loved has been a powerful panacea for the disease of desperately trying to 'fit in!'

5. Shop The Store

Don't just look in your section. The nature of a thrift store is that everything gets moved around a lot so you never really know where your lust-list items may show up.

Opshopulence is about being a rule breaker in the pursuit of unique style. Sure you might be a Miss but why can't you rock some Mr vibes? Or vice versa! Guys clothes look incredible on girls. It's a great way to achieve a more comfortable, relaxed fit for curves and *oui bien sur a French femme insousiance*. I know quite a few men—gay and straight who aren't afraid to shop the women's section either. Same goes for my trans and non-binary friends. They don't let one section define them.

This is the *haus* of whatever the hell goes.

Throw that size chart and department store restriction out the window, be fashion gender fluid—have fun and try it all! Half my wardrobe is from the men's section and I steal my hubby's clothes all the time.

Two other untapped sections I am a big fan of are sleepwear and haberdashery. Seriously, so much goodness here. Try a silky ¾ black slip as a dress under a leather biker jacket or turn it into a skirt by knotting a tee over the top. Butter-soft single color pajama shirts can look fantastic with denim. Don't get me started on the haberdashery... Ok, if I must! This is where a good ol' fashion craft-ernoon comes in, and the only limit is your imagination.

A well-stocked thrift store haberdashery section presents a world of quirk possibility for timeless tailored pieces. I scan the shelves for:

- **Embroidered tapestries:** Trust me, they can look incredible on the back of a jacket. Check out the unfinished tapestry (below) I reimagined for a thrift fashion runway. It still had the needle and thread in, so I took it as a sign to keep it to add to the one-of-a-kind factor. It's like a moment in time, an expression of art, and I totally love that.
- **Jars of joy:** I'm talking buttons, beads, pearls; I've even found shells and added them to a pair of summer slides using my trusty glue gun.

My embroidered tapestry DIY as featured in a thrifted fashion runway show

- **Trims and tassels:** Look for layers of ribbon, lace, feathers—you never know what you might find to add a dash of fabulous to the hem of a skirt or blazer cuff.
- **Fabric:** one-of-a-kind material is such a muse for me. It can be turned not only into a garment but also a chic scarf, top or asymmetrical panel. I uncovered the most incredible Egyptian cotton print from the '90s recently; it added a show-stopping element when I decided to create a Met Gala inspired look. I draped the fabric over one side of a vintage prom dress secured in place with a men's looped belt.
To this day it is my most liked Instagram post and is now the cover of this very book, beautifully illustrated by Lily Gerasimchuk.

A great testament to the perceived idea of 'waste' or 'scraps' if you ask me!

This is Opshopulence incarnate.

+ Prom dress base
+ Fabric draped over one shoulder
+ Cinched with a men's belt
+ Brooch cluster
+ Beloved wedding shoes

6. Sew Good

In the haberdashery section you'll also pick up pins, stitching and knitting needles, wool, cotton, zips—all the elements you need for attaching and fastening. Start collecting them so you can create a little DIY kit. I have a few jars at home that contain needle and thread, odd buttons, broken necklaces, cute patches, and bling paraphernalia—always handy to have on standby, should a craft-ernoon strike. My grandma taught me to hand stitch, and while I'm no dressmaker, it's a simple skill that certainly comes in handy when I need to attach, mend or switch. For the most part, that's all it takes to prolong the life of our clothes.

Highly recommend grabbing yourself a glue gun. A little bedazzling never hurt nobody! I explore the embellishment and fine details I see on street style and in the runway collections then challenge myself to create my own incarnation. A basic understanding of crafting passed on from Mum forms the basis of my approach, but I also dive into Pinterest, YouTube and Instagram for clever ideas to deconstruct and reconstruct the pieces I own.

7. Know Your Body

Know your style. Don't be a slave to the trends. Only buy what feels great and flatters you. Do it your way. This is why developing your personal or signature style is such an important factor towards your Opshopulence—the more in touch you are, the less you will need. While relaxed, loose denim shorts can be such a cute look on a surfer girl, I just can't go for that vibe. I'm more of a ¾ linen summer dress and handmade leather sandals sista. I know what works on me, what I will actually wear, and the things I feel most *me* in. Find the right canvas pieces for your shape and stick it to the fruit section of body analysis—no pears or apples here. You do you, boo boo!

8. Consistency Is Key

You don't just go to the gym once to build your biceps. Same goes for toning those thrifting muscles. Do it regularly and be consistent. Visit your local thrift stores as often as you can and remember you don't always have to buy. Just get among it, see what's there and dream up ideas. The more you explore, the more you increase your chances. New stock comes out every day. Go to them all, not just your local or the one you love the most.

People often ask me which thrift store is my favorite, and in all honesty my answer is *all* of them. Each thrift store has a different community, customer base and donation habits. It's also lovely to get to know the staff, and you can be sure that when you do you won't just form a beautiful sense of community, chances are they will keep you in mind for special pieces too.

9. Set A Good Tailor On Speed Dial

Maybe the unicorn Dior jacket you found has boxy shoulder pads, but if you have it altered, it will still be much less than the original price tag. Tracing back to my dad's time in London, all his clothes were bespoke and crafted with thought. This sensibility has stayed with me and I call on my trusty dressmaker Jan to regularly restyle my second hand finds to suit my shape to perfection. It's a great way to look more put together, expensive, and it will help you carry yourself with that Opshopulent pride because everything is in place.

10. Take A Tool Kit

You may call me a thrifting nerd but so be it! Seriously, I take snacks, water, a tape measure, inspiration pics, a wish list and reusable shopping bags. I even have a pocket magnifying glass, one of those amazing old school ones, to check fine hallmarks on jewels and brooches.

My kit always makes things run smoothly and more mindfully for me.

Before long, you'll be a regular Mary Poppin' tags too!!

CHAPTER SEVEN

30 Things to Thrift

This is my ultimate LUST-have list, and the items that keep me safe from the dreaded 'I have nothing to wears.' These are the canvas pieces I mentioned previously; the blank slates of style that will forever work and be fabulous, in my opinion.

A lot of them didn't start their life as fashion items, they were totally about function, and once you own them it's not hard to see why.

Kwabena Boake-Yiadom

1. White Button-Down

Where to begin with the beauty of this piece? Just as unbelievably practical and timeless as it is ripe for reinvention. I love wearing my husband's white collared shirts as a skirt embellishment. These are a cinch to find in a thrift store. Always head to the men's section for a sexier fit. Oversized is life, giving you all manner of ways to wear it: off the shoulder, backwards, collar popped, encrusted with brooches, cinched with a belt, layered with a vest or jacket, endless options.

2. Vintage Levis

Did you know denim was originally the chosen uniform of miners, laborers and welders? Copper rivets were applied to prevent pocket tear, orange double stitching for reinforcement, and they were the first to use the now coveted button fly. Jeans were named after the Italian city of Genoa, where cotton corduroy—called either jean or jeane—was manufactured. Well over a century after the fabric was patented by Levi Strauss and tailor Jacob Davis, jeans remain a treasured member of our wardrobes. Hollywood helped to glamorize these humble pants by putting them up on the big screen; seen on handsome cowboy types to coquettish 'It' girls like Bardot and, of course, bad boys such as Brando and James Dean giving them a very desirable proof of cool. The all-cotton versions are the classics and really do take great shape on your body. When you find the right fit, it's like a fashion fairy tale.

3. Black Blazer/Tux Jacket

Instant style and a fast-track to chic. Look for a sharp shoulder, solid tailoring and stand out details. I choose this item time and again to team with a t-shirt or belted over a vintage dress. It can do no wrong. If you like the cut but not the buttons, switch them out for something fancier like gold or brass military-style, that's one of my all-time super easy Opshopulence tricks.

4. Trench Coat

As the name suggests, these clever coats were originally created for soldiers in the trenches during WWI! Those extra pockets and purposeful fastenings were all about practicality. The belt had ID rings for hooking accessories, the caped back created a water drip-off solution, and the storm flap at the shoulder provided much needed ventilation. Both Aquascutum and Burberry take credit for having created the trench, but the truth is they really helped popularize an item that was already in circulation. Again, it was Hollywood that made the trench a hot-ticket item. Cue megastars like Bogart, Hepburn and Dietrich for giving it serious style cred. I have two—a softer more flexible version that is the most practical throw-on, and a more structured vintage thrifted Burberry piece perfect for a more polished affair. I live in both and constantly dress them up and down. They are such a staple for me, and I mourn the loss of wearing them when summer comes around!

5. Pencil Skirt

Sexy, flattering, and so much versatility. Team with a slinky silk cami and sandals during summer or combine with a belted jacket and heels when you mean business. I have a vintage wool wonder that skims my form, and a slightly stretch version which is great for a chic summer run around.

> 'I can't remember a time that I wasn't drawn to vintage. Whether it be clothing or accessories, vintage pieces have such a unique quality and their workmanship is second to none.'
>
> @shopportunityvintage

Emily @ekoluv in my Burberry trench, worn here inside out for a fresh take.

@joyebenspiff

6. Denim Jacket

Instant cool, great layering piece and an item I call on time and again. I have three! A super faded and distressed 1973 Levi find—it is so worn and tattered, but I love the dichotomy of teaming it with a pretty dress. Another one I have is black, super-oversized and slouchy with big pockets. The third denim jacket is a beautifully loved and comfy cropped number. Seen here encrusted with some of my beloved brooches.

7. White Tee

An incredible canvas piece that creates endless options. Casual, corporate, or even couture-inspired, this fashion icon can function in any form. Tucked in, tied in a knot, or just hanging loose, the white tee is a wardrobe wonder. My tip here is get one slightly oversized and roll up the sleeves. I wear men's as I don't like the mainstream cut of women's t-shirts. Men's tees are much better on the female form,

I find. Also consider the rock or slogan variant of the tee. They add instant character and quirk to an outfit especially when you wear a band you love. Led Zeppelin is my favorite and I nearly fainted when I found a vintage Zep tee at a street fair in NYC for $5! I always look for oversized, butter-soft, relaxed and worn-in then love to team it with a suit or pleated skirt for a great contrast.

8. Little Black Dress (LBD)

If it's good enough for Audrey Hepburn, the little black dress definitely gets an A+ from me too. I have a super versatile ¾-length stretch jersey ethical find from Lois Hazel (@loishazel), which I wore eleventy-thousand ways on my honeymoon and continue to do so now—and in all the seasons. To embrace the quirk side of my style mantra, I have an incredible black '80s prom dress that is surprisingly super wearable during winter. She has played many a time from Sydney to New York City, and looks amazing with heeled, lace-up boots and a leather biker jacket, or with combat boots and a denim jacket! Canvas pieces don't ever have to mean corporate Barbie boring!

The '80s prom dress holding her own at the Met Museum NYC, with my husband Lee

9. Little White Dress (LWD)

The lighter cousin of the LBD, little miss white dress is also surprisingly wearable. The perfect one is still on my thrift lust-list, actually. I would love linen or silk, maxi-style, loose and flowy but I think a firm-fitting version could be wonderful too. A LWD dress will go with so much! Put a slouchy sweater or belted blazer over her in winter, and tousled hair and a strappy sandal in summer. #**Swoon**

Emily in @ekoluv

@stylecrone

10. Vintage Blouse

They always have a unique print, cut and interesting proportion, tucked into high-waisted denim jeans or a pencil skirt will provide personality to an outfit with minimal effort. These babies quite often have beautiful buttons and divine details like shoulder pads, darting, disco collars or bows, which I am so here for. I have yellow silk, tiger print silk, plain cream silk and a handmade black and gold chain print which rocks very Versace vibes. My white sheer polka dot blouse is a big staple for me too.

> 'I buy a lot of vintage because, well, it's AMAZING! And truthfully you can get great stuff for not a lot of money. I have a passion for vintage clothing because of the quality and uniqueness of the pieces (you don't really have to worry about showing up in the same outfit as someone else).'
>
> Tracee Ellis Ross

11. Cashmere/Wool Sweater

Natural fibers are full-on luxury, they feel fabulous and make you look expensive. Plus they keep their quality and shape if cared for properly—pilling and pulling will be a thing of the past. If it isn't, I use this incredible sweater stone I found at eco-friendly brand Eileen Fisher in NYC, gentle on your clothes and the environment. It's essentially a pumice stone so if you don't have an Eileen Fisher store near you, you could just get one from your local pharmacy. Lightly run the pumice stone along the outside of your sweater (also works on shirts, jackets and pants) to quickly restore the surface to its former glory.

12. Black Skinny Jeans

Beyond handy and a wonderful building block for an outfit. Dressed up or down, they require minimal thinking and I'm all about that. Could be denim, leather, faux leather or good quality, thick leggings style.

13. Mom Jeans

There's nothing quite like a relaxed comfy pair of jeans. A high-waist, rolled-up cuffs and Converse high-tops or Doc boots, this style staple is the perfect off-duty dream girl.

14. Plaid Blazer

Contrast, texture and a cool attitude, especially the vintage incarnation. Try teaming with spots or stripes for a fun print clash. I also look for mine in the men's section of thrift stores. I much prefer the cut and oversized nature, looks incredible cinched or relaxed with a tee underneath, jeans and high-tops.

15. Animal Print

Zebra, tiger, snake, leopard—I love it all! If you ask me, it's a neutral. I have leopard print boots, scarves, a midi skirt and a blazer. I've lost count how many times I've worn them. I adore this vintage tiger blouse I found from a small local business, Telling Time Vintage @tellingtimevintage.

16. Breton Stripe Tee

So Frenchy, so chic and that sleeve is super flattering. Hey if it's good enough for style icon Brigitte Bardot!

17. Simple Black Knit/ Turtleneck

Timeless elegance and a great layering piece. Think Audrey Hepburn in *Roman Holiday*. I also love the turtleneck style in bodysuits. I have a black, nude, and brown python print.

'Thrift doesn't limit me to what's on trend. I don't care about trends, I care about what I like. Thrift shops have everything, not just trends of the moment. The items I thrift are my style. If you're dressing in your own unique style, you're never out of fashion anyway.'

Sabra @mystyleismybrand

18. Brooches

The world is a better place with bling! Former United States Secretary of State, Madeleine Albright even wrote a book about them! *Read my Pins* is an ode to how this A-game accessory 'became part of her personal diplomatic arsenal.' Not just a slice of her signature style, they grew into a political statement without her having to say a word. This is their power and I constantly seek out sparkly friends to add to my collection. I pin them to everything, a cluster on my jackets has developed into a definite 'Faye' fashion statement and they are always a great conversation starter. I also add them to: bralettes layered over a white button-down, corsets, dresses, t-shirts, soft fabric handbags, leather jackets, even shoes!

'Before long and without intending it, I found that jewelry had become part of my personal diplomatic arsenal. Former President George Bush had been known for saying "Read my lips"; I began urging colleagues and reporters to "read my pins."'

Madeleine Albright

19. Statement Earrings

Love an ear chandelier! Especially with a slick ponytail or soft waves, it just screams look-at-me chic no matter your age, shape or size.

20. Vintage Leather Boots

The way they were made, their lived-in appeal... I just love them! My favorite find to date are ¾ leather and suede lace ups with a definite nod to the Victorian era. Just divine and only $10! I've since seen high-street incarnations popping up everywhere. Choose a style that suits you, I promise they will be great friends. If you prefer new, there are so many ethical brands to choose from such as Australian label RM Williams, Everlane and Wootten, or hunt down a bespoke cobbler in your community. The Green Hub Brand Directory has some great suggestions to suit your feet and fashion lifestyle.

I also believe in the investment of a well-made designer pair. Prada or Gucci are particularly beautiful. I highly recommend having a look around the *TheRealReal* or *Vestiaire*, both pre-loved high-end portals filled with incredible second hand designer finds for half the price.

@loopistyle in elegant ethical fashion pieces from her own wardrobe

21. Corsets and Sleepwear

This is one of my ultimate styling elements. Underwear but make it outerwear. I have about seven corsets that I wear so often. They look fantastic under a men's suit, over a button-down (as pictured) or an oversized tee. Corsets have natural elements of couture—boning, cinching, structure—so they instantly elevate your look no matter your style. How amazing does Shaqaeq look dressed modestly with a corset? They know no boundaries.

Silk slips are another style legend. Great for concealing a see-through dress or skirt but also fantastic reimagined under a suit jacket, or with a t-shirt or denim jacket over the top. I always look in the sleepwear section of thrift stores and I very rarely use these pieces to sleep in! They are just too good to not go outside. I have also found some beautiful silk slips on Etsy.

@shaqaeqrezai

22. Nanna Bags

Boxy cuts, beautifully crafted, one-of-a-kind fixtures and finishings, it's such a great cheat sheet to an elevated look. I have bags made entirely from shells, shiny Perspex or the softest of Italian leather. They *all* look designer yet cost me next to nothing.

I customized this nanna bag using broken necklace pieces

@missvictoriaanthony

23. Scarves

Tie around your neck, on a bag handle for an *Hermès* ode, turn into a belt, wear as top, trim a ponytail... seriously don't get me started. My scarf collection continues to grow because they are just such fabulous little fashion helpers. Even my hubby has learnt the merits, rocking a chic cravat with a lot of his outfits now. **#soproud**

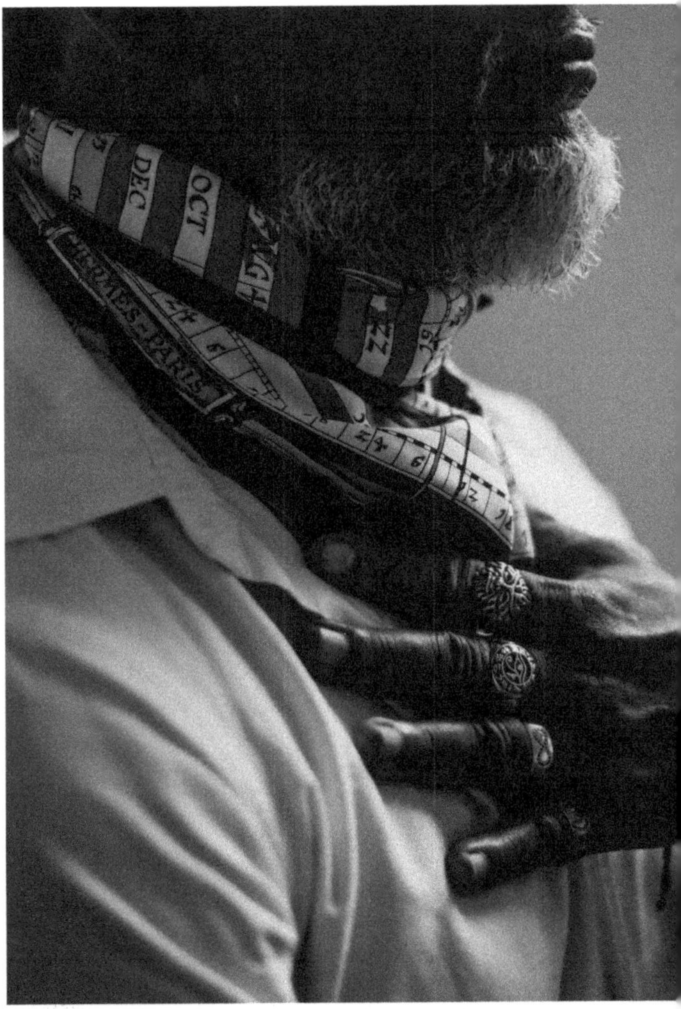

24. Midi Skirts

Old school cool and bonus points for **#pleatsplease**. The ¾ length is sexy minus the hooch, and they have such a feminine charm. I live in mine!

25. Hats

Go-to glamour! A hat is the crossing of your outfit 'T'—it finishes off a look just so. Faves of mine include an authentic Greek fisherman's cap, straw trilby, and Lee loves his felt Akubras.

26. One-of-a-kind Coat

I'm very blessed to have not only my dad's bespoke coats from London, but also my grandma's, and God bless her, it's leopard print. Praise be! These are walking, talking style stories and without fail will start up a yarn. That aside, they always make me feel special. Whether it be the unique color, unusual cut, or fantastic pattern, it's such a great expression of who you are without having to say a word.

Kaitlin @windycitythrifter

27. Leather Biker

Olivia Newton John knew the power of this staple piece was electrifying. They add instant cool and style cred to any ensemble. The more zips and buckles the better. I have two. One oversized (thrifted from the Salvos), the other is a conversion of three vintage jackets reimagined into a 'new to me' biker, actually modelled on the one Olivia wore in Grease! From a great store in Sydney called Fabrique Vintage (but it originally came from Paris).

28. Belts

These genius accessories have quickly become an integral part of my signature style. The smallest part of me is my waist so it's most flattering for me to highlight that. It also makes me look taller and totally like I know what I'm doing (even when I don't!). My tip here is wearing men's belts. I love the extra length for creating a designer inspired loop at the front. Honestly, it's like the frosting on my fashion cake! Vivienne Westwood and Alexander McQueen love extra-long belts but when I couldn't afford their price tag, I decided to get an extra-long men's belt for under $5 and DIY.

29. Sunglasses

Hide a multitude of sins while highlighting how cool you are! The cat's eye shape is my go-to but also a big fan of the classic aviator. You can find so many great pairs second hand.

@missvictoriaanthony in my beloved thrifted men's belt

30. Classic Suit

Apart from showing the world that you mean business, a two-piece is incredibly versatile. Try the blazer with jeans and heels, the pants with chic sneakers and a tee. The mix and match options are endless. When worn together, it's just so effortless yet extremely boss.

In all honesty there are at least 30 more I could add to this list. If you have a fave, tag me on Instagram **@fayedelanty** and share your most loved thrifted must-haves with me.

CHAPTER EIGHT

Let Reuse be your Muse
—Ready-To-Re-Wear

To kick us off here may I introduce you to the 5 Cs.

A quick and easy fashion reminder to get you to the Opshopulent side of town, stat!

These are simple styling tricks I find myself continuously gravitating towards because they are so effortless and effective.

My 5 Cs are:

Cinch in waists
Contrast fabrics and layer textures
Create lashings of statement bling
Collect beautiful buttons, trinkets and charms
Craft accessories into new looks

These are all elements you can tap into using what you already have (or they're super easy to find for a fraction of the price in a thrift store). Take a peek in your closet and see what you have: belts, scarves, different fabrics, accessories, and bling. Then try restyling and rethinking. You'll be amazed how items will feel 'new.'

Another thing I love to do is look at designer runway shows and muse on how I might be able to recreate some of the looks or elements of the looks by being a crafty little minx. An embellished shoulder, clashing prints, the fall of fabric or the way a belt is styled just so... I ask myself could I... *ditch buy for DIY, get wise and customize, make-do and mend!?*

I find quite often there is a clever way to *make more out of less...more or less!*

@dinischantelle in my @salvosstores ode to Alexander McQueen, Revive Festival 2019. This creation became part of a sustainability exhibition at the Queensland Museum in 2021

Top 10 Tips to Thrift Like an Eco-Stylist

1. Be Your Own Designer

Sure, take inspiration from the runway shows and what you see among the fashion magazines and editorials, but then make it your own. Muse on how you might like to interpret what you see for your own unique expression. How could you make it feel good for you and your lifestyle?

For me, it's definitely about the designer-inspired details on classic thrift pieces.

It's eye catching but effortless.

An oversized men's tux is transformed with a cinched waist and silk scarves cascading from the side (tucked under the belt) to create a dynamic asymmetrical panel. So easy, so inexpensive but so effective. For every-day Opshopulence, it's as simple as a vintage brooch on a white button-down or a beautiful vintage belt on a free-flowing maxi dress.

Shape-shifting second hand is such a passion for me!

> 'Second hand clothing has given me the freedom to be me in my unique way, to influence others to want to do the same and to be kind to the environment knowing that I won't find anybody else with my exact pieces, knowing I'm my own designer and giving me the freedom to wear whatever, whenever, with pride.'
>
> @styleaffiar_ruth

2. Stay Open

I screen-shot looks I love and take them with me when I go thrifting. This really helps to define what you are looking for and will serve as great inspiration for creating designer looks for less.

Pinterest is never far away either; however, I always leave room for my *re*imagination to take over. You truly never know what you will find at a thrift store, so while I might have a vision in mind, I love that this can totally be flipped on its fashion head when a magical, unexpected muse presents itself. It could be an incredible texture or color that takes me somewhere, and it's so fun to roll with it.

3. Start Simply

I get it, thrift stores can be overwhelming. So my advice is to start simply. Treat it like a normal shopping experience. Be discerning. Don't just buy a bunch of stuff because it's inexpensive, you'll just become a second hand hoarder! Begin by only looking for great quality classic items like a beautiful black jacket, a good pair of jeans, a simple tee or an LBD. Gain your thrifting confidence first and build from there.

> 'To me, looking expensive is how I put myself together. I mainly gravitate towards well-made and classic pieces. Which is what I thrift. There is an abundance of second hand quality pieces available. Why purchase brand new when my thrifted items look much better than some brand-new retail items!?'
>
> @mylove4vintage114

4. Hunting Instinct

Goodies are everywhere so it really pays to look around. Treat it like a *treasure hunt*! For me, there is no rhyme or reason as to which section I should go to first. I feel like each store tells me once I head in. Trust your fashion intuition and be guided to what you're drawn to. Having said that, the men's section, the $2 or clearance rack and the returns rack near the change room are a fave of mine. I love to touch the clothes, feel the fabrics, and connect with how it might be a worthy creation for me and my style expression.

> 'Thrift has opened my eyes to new possibilities; reimagination, reinvention, upcycling. Giving second hand pieces a new lease on life. When I see a trend or a piece I want, rather than rushing into a purchase, I add it to my thrift list. This allows me time to slow down and mindfully purchase in a more sustainable way. Keep your eyes and your mind open, because when you thrift, you never know what you'll find. It is not only good for the planet, but it's also an economical choice to make.'
>
> Lauren @lalunawolf.vintage

5. Think Outside the Style Square

Just because a scarf is traditionally for around the neck doesn't mean it can't moonlight as a wrap-around top secured with a fancy belt. Same goes for a long sheer vest. Maybe it could become a layer over pants or even an asymmetric side panel. I just see so much possibility, and op shops allow you to play. Price and perception aren't a priority. Freedom of expression is. Ignite your inner child and see what you can create together.

'Every single piece of clothing and accessories in every person's wardrobe is a designer piece. Each article's beginnings came from an idea of a designer regardless if it's mass produced or a one-off piece. If people just disregarded the $$ signs and embraced how the article made you feel wearing it, giving you confidence within yourself, we would not have a class war about fashion.'

@my_vintage_unicorn

@stylecrone

6. Try DIY

A simple black pencil skirt reinvented with a feather trim takes it next level. Old buttons can be glue-gunned onto a sweater to up the style stakes or why not distress your own jeans? You don't have to be a professional seamstress, there are so many simple DIYs you can try. 'No Sew' is a favorite search phrase of mine. Jump online and explore!

3 super easy Starter DIYs:
(head to **opshopulence.com** to watch my how-to videos)

Crop
1. Crop a cotton men's button-down/collared shirt at the waist
2. Keep the bottom half as well
3. Throw both pieces in the washing machine
4. Wear the top half with high-waisted skirts or over dresses
5. Use the bottom half as a corset teamed over a t-shirt, cinch and hold in place with a belt

Do the same with jeans. Crop the cuffs, keep the off-cuts, throw it all in the machine. Wear jeans as is but use the left-overs as cool cuffs on other blouses or jackets. I use rubber bands or sleeve garters to hold them in place around my wrist and create an exaggerated bell/tulip sleeve.

Tie
1. Head to your local craft store and grab two meters of satin ribbon in your chosen color
2. Pick a pair of your fave stilettos or flats
3. Tie the ribbon around the ankle straps and create serious bow drama

Iron-on
1. Grab some iron-on patches or glam motifs like angel wings from Etsy or eBay
2. Iron onto an old jacket to give a new lease on life

> 'We need to rethink the way we use our clothes and relove the discarded.'
>
> @style_travel_chic

> 'I've had people think I had a designer wardrobe when I was wearing discount threads.
> Attitude and a good tailor will take you far.'
>
> @mystyleismybrand

7. Divine Details

Always look for special trimmings. Gold buttons, heavy zippers, great tailoring, designer-inspired hardware. All these elements can either mean 'designer find' or they can be a tool you use to create a designer-inspired outfit. And if you love the tailoring of an item but it doesn't have these, then add them yourself. There is so much sublime story woven into the seams of second hand clothes, and it feels like such a luxury to be a part of that circular journey.

> 'I love vintage clothes because they have a story. I often like to imagine who owned them before me. Then I become part of that history as well. The story is so much more important than the brand or how expensive it once was. I especially love handmade pieces I find at the thrift store. I imagine the love and care that went into that article of clothing.'
>
> @milwaukeemuse

8. Restyle, Reinvent & Reimagine

I see the clothes as so much more than just garments on hangers. I love to see how far I can take it to recreate them. I cinch in waists, layer like it's a sport, tuck, twist, reshape, restyle and reimagine Use your designer inspo pics and see what you can refashion. The only limit is your imagination, and I think this is such a powerful way to take control of your personal style destiny. Don't be dictated to. Be your own goddamn muse!

> 'I love how second hand style has allowed me to express myself through clothing the way I've always dreamed of.'
>
> @styledbyempris

9. Tailor Made

Find yourself a good tailor and have those pieces you love altered to fit. I once found a DIOR Homme jacket for $10. The shoulder pads were a little too gridiron player for me and the sleeve was slightly long, but a quick tweak from my dressmaker Jan and I had the most amazing designer jacket to add to my wardrobe. Better yet, teach yourself to do it.

> 'I grew creative, went thrifting and with a pair of scissors and a sewing machine I made my own clothes. "Fake it til you make it" and this began the birth of my love for thrifting.'
>
> @twiggynchic

10. Rotate & Donate

Keep your wardrobe moving and don't hold onto to pieces you aren't wearing. Donate them, gift, share or swap. My rule is, if I bring 'new' finds in, then the equal amount has to go out.

Don't hold on to things that may only hold you back. Free up space for 'new to you' expression to come in seamlessly. There can be such beauty in the law of letting go.

> 'In my humble opinion, circular fashion makes the world go 'round.'
>
> @loopistyle

Opshopulence
Style Short Cuts

Embellish with vintage brooches

I am all about that bling. It's a fast-track way to fab-ify your look. A simple all-black ensemble will really pop with a beautiful dash of fashion frosting. I may have curbed my clothing dependency but I doubt the brooch obsession will ever be beaten; they are just so darn handy. Every op shop or second hand haven I visit, I seek out the brooch section. I am slowly building my collection, and yes Marie Kondo, they sure do spark joy! Try them on a lapel, to fasten a collar, add creativity to a cuff, haute couture a hat, give a designer-inspired element to a handbag. These purposeful little pins offer endless possibilities.

> 'For me, brooches are like tattoos; they say so much about you without saying anything at all. Each one tells a different story.'
>
> @rosiemae27

Customize

Patches, pretty jewels, or even personalized monogramming. These are all fantastic elements to add one-of-a-kind quirk to your ensembles. I love patches on denim, sparkly gems for shoes or an evening clutch. I'm a big fan of adding embossed initials to leather belts or embroidery to fresh white cotton. I aim to seek out local small makers for this kind of work. In my local area I've found an embroidery family who's been in business for 25 years. I take my op shop items to Lucy, her daughter Julia, and canine site manager, Cookie, for something special. It could be my name or a special quote or phrase and they are happy to do small runs. I look to fashion and then use my own contacts and creativity to design something no one else will have.

Wear a chic necktie

Make like a '50s French movie star and sport one of the quickest style tricks in the book. Scarves add that certain *je ne sais quoi* which speaks volumes. My husband Lee is a huge fan of them too, turning them into cravats. I found this authentic Hermès silk scarf in a $1 bin! I just bought it because I loved the print; it wasn't until a month later I realized what it was.

Rock bold statement earrings and a bright red lip

You can have the simplest of outfits and these two super-fast tricks will take you to fashion nirvana. Ear candy speaks elegance and attention to detail, a slick of striking fire engine on your kisser is sexy!

A messy side bun under a chic hat

Stylish, sure but also a sneaky trick to hide a multitude of sins including a week's worth of dry shampoo. Seriously, I get compliments all the time when I do this; if only they knew the chaos underneath!

Invest in shoes and bags you will cherish

I have some beautiful designer accessories like my Christian Louboutin wedding shoes that I wear over and over with denim and vintage dresses. My Louis Vuitton and Valentino bags come in so handy and continue to chic-up an outfit season after season.

You can find amazing shoes in op shops too. Enter my never been worn Manolo Blahniks I scored for $25 USD when I lived in NYC. I swear the style-angels sang (or maybe that was just me!). I may or may not have worn them cooking that night and watching TV in my midtown apartment. Check out pre-loved consignment stores, bricks and mortar, and online portals like *Vestiaire* or the *Real Real* for example. You will find beautiful lightly-worn designer accessories for half the price! Same goes for designer handbags.

On the flip side of this you can absolutely create a designer feel with thrift shop bags. One of my favorite things to do is to keep an eye out for designer inspired and vintage bags with one of a kind decadent hardware like a square handle, gold chain or expensive looking embellishment. Then I take them to my local bootmaker to have my initials embossed or do that as a gift for friends. This gives these pre-loved items such a fancy edge that everyone is fooled into thinking it's designer. If the fabric allows it, try adding a brooch where a designer logo would usually be for another touch of Opshopulence!

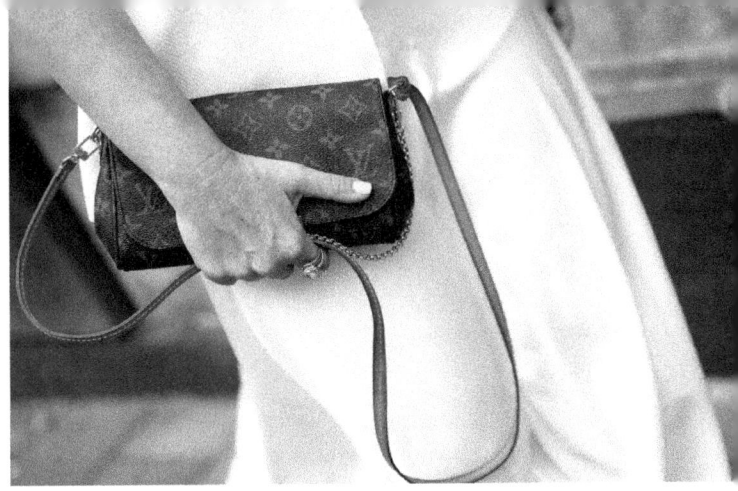

Vintage clothing and accessories

Garments from different eras will give you a one-of-a-kind quirk that you would never find in mainstream stores. Think a 1970s' band tee teamed with a sharp blazer, a pretty floral dress contrasted beside a cool 'nanna bag' and beaten-up biker boots. I always find items like this start conversations too.

Convert/Reuse/Reimagine

'The art of creating, up-cycling and reusing has been a passion and hobby of mine since I was a child. To imagine something unique from what would have ordinarily been discarded, and take it to the next level is such a creative outlet and hugely satisfying for me.

We all love a little bit of luxe in our life, but vintage designer clothing and accessories which are adorned with a fantastic variety of buttons and zipper pulls, like all of our clothes, sadly don't last. So once the fabric has worn out and can no longer be worn, what happens to these ornate embellishments which are still in such great condition?

Well I give them a new lease on life as unique jewellery items. I elevate them and reuse these fabulous pieces to make luxe for less sustainable jewellery. I use these designer remnants as pendant charms for necklaces, earrings, bracelets and brooches.'

Kimberley @shopportunityvintage

DESIGNER
Re-Designed

As modeled by some of my beautiful friends from around the globe using preloved clothing, clever tricks and what they already had in their wardrobes.

HOW TO THRIFT A CHANEL LOOK

1. Boucle blazer
2. White t-shirt
3. Slim-leg blue denim
4. Pearls
5. Fisherman's cap

Emily @ekoluv

Victoria @missvictoriaanthony

VERSACE FOR VERY LITTLE

1. Versace inspired print
2. Brooches and gold bling
3. Black stilettos
4. Chain accessories like necklaces or belts

@thefashionchase @staygoldengirl

Designer inspired style in unison thanks to my Nashville second hand highnesses, Elizabeth and Shana.

A Versace and Chanel mash up that packs a mega thrift punch.

All found in the girls' wardrobes.

A TOTAL MCQUEEN

1. Start with a classic black canvas
2. Cinch a shirt dress or duster coat
3. Statement corset belt and show stopper choker

Judith Boyd

'I have been shopping at estate sales, vintage shops, and yard sales since the 1970s. I had a friend who owned a vintage store in the 70s as well. What I discovered is that I loved the designs and look of vintage, and I wore it everywhere, including work. I became captivated with finding treasures and the thrill of the hunt. Cost was a factor, but not the most important part of wearing second hand. I found that I could express myself with authenticity and develop my own style by experimenting with different eras to create an individual look. This was when my adoration for headwear began.

Over the decades I learned about climate change and how buying new had a negative impact on the environment. My love for second hand became a political statement. Not only was preloved clothing my preference, it was also a way that I could contribute to the greater good as the climate crisis becomes more of an emergency with each passing day.

I started blogging in 2010 and added other social media platforms, such as Instagram, over the years. A large part of my message has been about creating ensembles with pieces acquired at vintage, thrift, and consignment shops. It's important for me to communicate my values and support the community of others who are second hand advocates online. Sustainability has become a lifestyle, a daily practice, and one of many ways to walk lightly on the planet.'

@stylecrone

'I began seeing the value in thrift through the thrifters I follow on Instagram. I noticed they had many cool, unique, and quality pieces that were all thrifted; the kind of items that I had been longing for. I bought my first piece in 2018; it was a leather Ralph Lauren vest. I couldn't believe that someone would part with such an awesome item that was in mint condition. I am a huge fan of Ralph Lauren quality and fit. The thought that I could acquire my most desired items for a small fraction of the cost is what first intrigued me.

In 2019 I became conscious of the real benefits of thrift. The environmental benefits resonated strongly with me as I was already an avid recycler, and water conservationist. I had never explored the connection between my shopping habits and the environment. Although I was not a consumer of fast-fashion, my consumption habits were not as intentional as they could have been.

After I started to thrift, my style became more of a reflection of who I really am. Thrift allowed me to express my style in ways that I was never able to before. I always knew that the retail stores were not selling what I really wanted during their seasons, but I didn't know how to find what I was really looking for. Unique, specific pieces from all eras was what I was looking for, and I found that through thrift.

During this same time my mother had become a thrifter/reseller as a retirement hobby. Her niche is jewelry and home décor. Thrift has allowed me to bond with her, and she loves finding, and gifting me the finishing touches to my styling. My mom has a real eye for jewelry and brooches. She does much better than I would ever do on my own.

If you haven't begun thrifting but want to, I would suggest staying open-minded. There are mint condition and excellent quality pieces to be found. Additionally, you will find your own true style through thrifting. I would also recommend trying online thrift. I initially found thrift stores to be overwhelming and intimidating. Online thrift is very well organized and easier to shop.

The suit is a grey flannel Ralph Lauren suit. Suits are classic, but I made it less traditional by pairing it with a ruffle bodice white cotton shirt. The gold accents really make it my own. Most people would have worn black shoes, but the gold belt, shoes, jewelry and brooch cluster add something eye-catching and unexpected. I felt that the look was really cool, but could be better. That's when I added the scarf at the waist. This is a styling trick I learned watching Faye. I can't even express how much the scarf elevated this overall look. I felt amazing when I finished styling it.'

Sabra @mystyleismybrand

CONSCIOUS COUTURE

1. Re-use
2. Re-think
3. Re-imagine

> 'Four old Zara dresses found on eBay converted into one giant conscious couture dress... to make the point that discarded fashion can be converted to create totally unique luxury with zero impact to the planet.
>
> In fact, this is a regenerative act, saving the cast aside from the trash and a life in landfill.
>
> Conversion is a huge part of the environmental solution'.
>
> Kate McGuire

@convertedcloset

BURBERRY LOOK

1. Classic trench coat (I turned this one inside out!)
2. LBD
3. Simple strap open-toe heel
4. Layer a chic scarf and belt over the top
5. Want to take it next level? Try this simple restyle with a scarf tucked into the belt

BAG LADY

Simple DIY ideas to bling up a second hand tote, clutch or backpack.

1. Wrap a scarf around the handle à la Hermès
2. Scour Etsy for designer-inspired patches and embellish
3. Pin brooches to create designer-inspired effects
4. Play with paint and pens. Why not try splashing a black patent leather clutch with flecks of white paint? (Place clutch atop newspaper, dip brush, then flick onto item for a splattered artistic effect.) You could also try a graffiti-inspired effect by doodling onto a similar clutch, words like: reuse, reinvent, etc. Its very 'Street' Opshopulence! Think Louis Vuitton/Stephen Spratt collab but *thrift savvy*
5. Use broken necklaces and old bits of jewelry (simply attach using a glue gun)

SAVVY STYLE HACKS

Short, super clever tricks to fast-track your way to Opshopulence!

- Earrings can also be used as brooches; simply pierce the fabric with the earring rod/arm and secure with the earring back. Clip-on earrings and trinkets can also be glued onto giant gold safety pins (easily found on Etsy, eBay or Amazon) to create a Versace-esque brooch adornment. (See Instagram reels **@fayedelanty**)
- Get rid of the old smell by airing in the sun for a few days. Spray with a mixture of a few drops of clove oil and water. (Spot test first with delicate fabrics like silk.)

Launder tip

Wash all the clothes you thrift before wearing them or air them in the sun to naturally disinfect. Make sure items are clean and laundered before you donate them.

Consider a GUPPY bag for synthetic materials.

DID YOU KNOW?

'Every time we wash our clothes, tiny fibers particularly from synthetics like acrylic, nylon and polyester, break off. Waste water treatment plants can't filter these tiny fibers efficiently and so they will find their way into our streams, rivers and oceans.

The tiny fibers that end up in the water concentrate pervasive bacteria and pollutants and are consumed by aquatic organisms, which can result in gastrointestinal infections and blockages, reproductive problems, and starvation—problems that ultimately work their way up the food chain. Which means we end up ingesting it too!

Microfibers are now the most abundant form of plastic pollution in our oceans but what can a single person do?

The Guppyfriend was developed to offer a pragmatic yet effective measure to put a stop to the microfibers pollution and to raise awareness for the problem. Pop your clothes into the bag that contain synthetic materials and simply wash with your other clothes. The Guppyfriend will catch all the microfibers that break off during the washing cycle; it will protect and extend the life of your clothes too.'

seashepherd.org.au

For leather items like vintage belts, I've actually unintentionally left them out in the rain on my window sill then dried them in the sun and the smell completely vanished!

A brooch is a style chameleon. Clip it on a jacket, jeans, bag, shoes, hat or even a t-shirt for stand-out style. Bonus points for a cluster of them on a garment. I think this can look super chic.

> Worried about marking your clothes by pining on brooches? Paint the pin with clear nail polish.

T-shirt too long? Snip the hem and the sleeves yourself for a cool customized effect. Keep the scraps and use them as scrunchies, hair ties or cleaning rags that can be washed and reused.

Don't spend hundreds on distressed denim. Thrift a pair and shred them yourself. All you need is a pair of scissors, a cheese grater (seriously!), and your washing machine will do the rest.

Contradict dress codes. Try sequins in the day with army fatigues. Leather with lace. Corsets with t-shirts. Ripped denim with a structured jacket and a stylish brooch cluster.

Take basic black to bling town. Simply drape a scarf around the back of your neck, secure either side at the front with a fabulous belt.

Create fashion drama over a pair of jeans and a jacket by adding an eye-catching asymmetrical panel.

All you need is a belt, brooch, scarf or striking material. Grab one end of the scarf and let the rest hang vertically underneath your hand, pin a brooch through the top and secure to the side of the hip area on what you're wearing. Leave as is or add a belt on top.

Borrow from the boys. Men's band tees, white or stripe button-downs and suits can look super sexy on girls. I even wear my husband's collared shirts as a skirt—all I do is tuck them into or over a belt.

Try this easy DIY with two shirts. Use two men's collared shirts of different patterns or colors—button the left side of one to the right side of the other, drape across your back, do the other buttons up at the front. Tie the arms around your waist to create a cinched-in effect.

Transform a t-shirt by adding a lace trim onto the hem or snipping the sleeves and stitching in a contrasting fabric like sequins or Boucle.

Look for jars of old mix-and-match buttons in op shops. They can be an incredible way to embellish a sweater, pair of pants, a skirt or a bag. Pick tonal colors you like, arrange clusters and simply glue-gun them on. Embellishment like this has been seen time and again on catwalks, particularly with brands like Mui Mui and Prada.

My husband's shirts SKIRT

EVERYDAY OPSHOPULENCE

Let's take a look at timeless style icons, and how you can easily thrift their looks. What all these fashion legends have in common is how they make everyday style items incredibly luxe. Button-downs, high-waisted denim, simple tees, structured blazer, white sundresses. Opshopulence doesn't have to be difficult. There are so many beautiful ways to work it into your everyday. If COVID equipped us with anything, it's that there is power in simplicity. We all appreciate style, comfort and ease within our wardrobe. I definitely did my fair share of sweats wearing. I just found super quick ways to elevate how these items made me feel. A slick of lippy, a sparkly brooch, sometimes earrings or throwing on a chic blazer and my Doc Marten boots if I had to go to the shop for supplies.

Explore these style icons; it's all the simple pieces that make their star power shine even brighter.

Audrey Hepburn: fitted black jeans, ballet flats, and a turtleneck.

Keith Richards: distressed white tee, print suit jacket with attitude like leopard or zebra, beat up/relaxed denim, long scarf, boots.

Anita Pallenberg: The Ultimate Bohemian babe—flowy dresses, luxe vintage fur coats and bold boots.

Robert Plant: slogan tee, fitted denim, flowing hair.

Jane Birkin: simple white t-shirt, high-waisted jeans, raffia bag.

Brigitte Bardot: Lace blouse, jeans, tousled hair, pout.

Kira @thegreenhub_

How To Build An Ethical Wardrobe

What is an ethical wardrobe exactly, I hear you ask? Well, this is what mine looks like:

- 70% Op shop clothing
- 10% Designer/investment pieces
- 10% Vintage garments
- 10% Ethical brands—a few of my personal favorites are Lois Hazel, Muse the label and Adidas for workout gear, who have a recycled plastic range now.

If I have anything from the high-street or mainstream retailers, it would be accessories like earrings, scarves, stockings and underwear.

I aim for progress not perfection and shop my wardrobe's contents as much as possible over hitting the stores and buying something, constantly challenging myself to create 'new looks' from what I already have. I review my wardrobe regularly to see what I'm really wearing and what's just sitting there. I either pass it on to a friend, swap it or donate it. You may think I have a huge walk-in with bundles of clothes, but guess what? I actually just have one small white cupboard with half a meter hanging space and four shelves that I work really hard to keep neat, minimal and functional. Such a far cry from my excessive more is more days. I actually get overwhelmed now if it becomes too full. A cull will always calm me down!

Apart from its contents being sourced responsibly, I have also committed to making it sustainable for my lifestyle too.

'Sustainability has to be sustainable for you.'

Dr Anita Van Dyke @rocket_science

For me, that means not too cluttered, easy to navigate and never stocked with stuff for the sake of stuff. I aim to have the bulk of it well-fitting and functional but of course with a little bit of room for fun and whimsy. Committing to this decluttered state helps my peace of mind and creativity. Even when I travel now, I very rarely take check-in luggage. I just hate having too much to carry—I feel it clutters me mentally. This has been a natural development for me as I learnt to meditate and saw that so much of the material matter I thought I needed was in fact weighing me down.

My minimal wardrobe space

7 Steps to a Conscious Closet

Step 1. Take stock

Literally! Get in there and go through everything. Pull out the pieces you definitely wear on the regular—for me that's jeans, midi skirts, tuxes and tees and maxi dresses. Put them aside and give them a once over to see if anything needs repairing or cleaning.

Step 2. Be honest

What are you not wearing? What haven't you worn for a while? Ask yourself why?

Is it uncomfortable, impractical, ill-fitting, out of fashion? Be tough on yourself, otherwise it's just stuff taking up space and, trust me, that will eventually stress you out. On the flip side, is it an item you would wear if it was mended? Could it be a simple tweak, tailor or embellishment to make it cool again? If so put it in the FIX pile.

Step 3. Time to let go

With the pieces you are definitely not wearing, why not donate them to a charity? Your fashion could do wonders for someone else and that's a great element to consider when you notice you're having trouble releasing your grip. Is it serving you or could it really assist someone else? Do make sure its good quality though, something that you would feel good about giving to a friend. If it's not up to scratch, look for the local textile recycling options in your neighborhood. A simple Google or a chat to your council will guide you the right way.

Step 4. Shop your stash

Have some fun dreaming up new ways to wear what you already have. Google 'beige blazer street style', for example, and check out all the inspo for a new take on your tired piece. Doing this always gives me a new-found love for my old items. Also consider customizing. Check out the trends and see what simple techniques you could apply to clothing you already have. Perhaps some vintage patches on a denim jacket, a chic feather trim or fancy new buttons. A little reinvention goes a long way.

Step 5. Lust-list

So what's missing in your wardrobe that you really need? A great blazer for work, more cool tees, or dresses? My first port of call is to always hit my local thrift store and look for those items there. I guarantee you'll definitely find some of the things you're looking for. Op shops are such a good penny and planet-saving option.

Step 6. Eco-luxe

What you can't find thrifting hit up vintage and ethical stores in your area. Look for great vintage band tees, one-of-a-kind dresses, belts and scarves. Check out **@thegreenhub_** for some great suggestions on ethical brands to explore. Kira has guides for everything from sweaters, swim, sexy dresses to socks and more.

Step 7. Slow and steady

Ethical fashion finds. I'm so happy to take my time and do the research for the brands I really believe in. Case in point: a little black dress. I struggled to find this in a charity shop; I knew the exact kind of cut I wanted but I just didn't see it there. I researched online and Instagram looking at ethical Australian brands I resonated with. Enter Lois Hazel. She made the most perfect ¾ cotton-rib dress that legit saved my life on our honeymoon. I wore it constantly in multiple ways and continue to do so now. It felt great to put power into my purchasing and choose a brand that really aligned with Mother Nature and my values. We all have the power to do this. Vintage clothing is an incredible option for one-of-a-kind quality chic too.

> 'Vintage clothing is a generic term for garments originating from a previous era. True vintage begins from 20 years ago and goes all the way to 100, after which time it becomes an antique. Vintage clothes reflect the styles and trends of the era they represent. Retro—short for retrospective—usually refers to clothing that imitates the style of a previous era. Reproduction (or repro) clothing is a newly-made copy of an older garment.'
>
> Wikipedia

@convertedcloset

Fabrique Vintage is one of my favorite preloved emporiums, read on for divine wisdom from co-owner Ruth Orblin.

At Fabrique Vintage, it's possible to see and touch pieces as old as 1900, right alongside denim jackets, shirts and jeans that are only 20 years old. It's difficult to illustrate with words the difference between the fabric we know today compared with what was being produced in the first half of the 20th century, but without this context my customers would not be able to learn to appreciate for themselves the value of the vintage we sell. It empowers people to look for themselves at the details of what they wear: what kind of fabric it is, how the stitching is done, what the shape represents (i.e. where it fits in an historical context), and to be able to discern between different levels of quality, both of the fabric and the garment itself. This kind of knowledge empowers customers when they leave my store and continue to consume elsewhere, it helps them place a value for themselves on what they consume.

We feel that it is really important to keep old and rare pieces so that we can bring people deeper into the vintage culture when they visit our store. By bringing denim pieces of many styles and ages, this narrative can be filled out with real examples in the minds of our clients. We find it really brings pleasure to the experience when clients are able to visit the store and to see and touch things they have never seen before, and at the same time to be able to contextualise those pieces into their personal knowledge and to fill out that wisdom a little with the extra knowledge that we are able to share with them.

There are many people who want to jump off the train of fast fashion, not only because it hurts the wallet to replace the wardrobe every season but because it is a large portion of their personal consumption. The reality is that the large vintage clothing dealers in the world already hold more clothes than Zara or H&M will make in a year, five years even.

> *In addition to this, the intrinsic value of vintage clothing is already higher because it is manufactured at a much higher quality than what we can buy today for a relative price. And we really don't need to be producing so many new garments – certainly not in the quantity that is currently occurring.*
>
> *There is an abundance of fabric ready to be reused and repurposed.*

5 Tips to tell it's vintage

In the words of Rachel Lynch

In my opinion, tags are the easiest way for a beginner to work out if something is vintage. These are some of my simple tips and elements to look for to uncover the vintage finds.

1. **Country of manufacture:** Vintage clothes pre-dating the 90s will predominantly be made in the country you have just found them in. Most clothing didn't travel far back in the day, so most countries produced their own clothing. Look for 'Made in Australia', 'Made in NZ', 'Made in the U.S.'. It is very uncommon to find genuine vintage clothing made in China or India.
2. **Font:** Vintage tags are always far more elaborate than sleek modern tags. Look out for large, ornate tags with interesting fonts, colors and images.
3. **Care Instructions:** Look for tags that have very simple care instructions such as 'Cold Wash' 'Dry Clean Only.' Vintage clothing tags will rarely have care symbols on them as they were introduced in the late 90s.
4. **Material tags:** The material composition will normally be mentioned on the main tag of vintage items or be on another tag attached to the main tag. Very rarely will you find a material tag on a side seam as you do in modern garments. Also note the types of fabrics commonly used in vintage garments: 'crimplene,' 'terylene,' 'lurex,' 'rayon,' 'nylon.'

5. **Sizing**: Clothing pre-dating the 70s in Australia will not have numbers to indicate sizes but letters instead. SSW=Slim Small Woman; SW=Small Woman; XW=Extra Woman. When looking at later vintage that does have numerical sizing you will notice that, generally speaking, the size will be 'incorrect' by roughly two sizes. A size 16 on a vintage tag will fit a modern size 12.

Mindfully Wed

I married the love of my life, Lee, on December 22, 2017. Back then, there wasn't much talk about sustainable weddings, but I really wanted to walk the talk and extend what I was doing in my every-day to my holy matrimony. I didn't really know where to start, but I put my beagle nose to the ground and got to researching. Here's what I uncovered. Lee and I even made it on the tele and in the UK papers!

Daily Mail article (Taken from my blog Sept 2017)

The Dress

This is the ultimate wear-once item, so I wanted to find a way to make it more mindful. Enter Lenka Couture—Australia's first ethically-accredited bridal couture designer. Lenka and I designed my dress from scratch using existing designer dead-stock left-over lace and ethically sourced, small run, silk satin to create my one-of-a-kind eco-dream-dress.

The left-over lace came from a high-end bridal designer and was considered scraps! We acquired the divine Italian-made cotton lace in three bits for $50! It was originally $500 a meter. We made my bridesmaid dresses using the same organic silk-satin as my dress, and the coolest element is that we naturally dyed them with brown onion skins, yep onion skins! Once heated and boiled in water the brown onion skins release a copper/coral/dusty pink tone that is just to DYE for. And *no* it doesn't smell. More on how to DIY below. It's so easy. I had seen the color I loved on a dress that wasn't made ethically and it was expensive so I thought surely there must be a way to create my own environmentally-friendly version, et voila!

The Flowers

I had no idea about this, but when I was on a pre-eco wedding shoot, I discovered that a lot of the wedding flowers and the ones we buy from markets or florists have been flown from overseas. How do they last? Sadly, with lots of chemicals and a big carbon footprint to get them here. It blew my mind to discover the **slow flower movement**—bouquets that are foraged, locally grown, and even reused. Vanessa from **@dancing_blossom_studio** is doing seriously cool things with **#GrownNotFlown**. I'm really glad I discovered this concept in time to add it to our wedding values. Vanessa picked me elements from her area and her parents' farm, she grew me others and even added in divine touches that were intrinsic to Lee and me—feathers and crystals. She did this on the buttonholes for Lee's groomsmen too.

Confetti

My mum reduced me to happy tears when she told me she'd been collecting leaves and flowers all year from her garden and her travels. Then using a $2 butterfly shaped hole punch, she made me eco-friendly confetti that breaks down, returning to the earth afterwards. Genius, right?

Cars

Man, they can rip you off deluxe here! We asked a couple of our friends with nice cars to drive us, and then we used Uber X. My lovely friend Adrian drove Dad and me in his beautiful Mercedes, and he added so many heartfelt touches that made me cry, again!

Make-up and Hair

I called on friends I work with to help me. They gave me mate's rates, which was so very kind and they used ethical products where possible.

The Boys

Lee wore suede desert boots sourced from Australian label, Country Road. A Ralph Lauren white button-down thrifted from the Salvos. We bought Lee's suit new, but I cannot tell you how many times both he and I have worn it again.

The Rings

We had such a divine experience sourcing my engagement ring. I'm a self-confessed fussy Libran, so Lee knew that it would be best if we could design the ring together. This also allowed us to take the time and choose a merchant who had an ethical mindset. Affinity Diamonds were incredible; they searched for months to find me the perfect conflict-free dream pear-shaped black diamond, and in a beautiful slice of serendipity it ended up coming from NYC, which is our spiritual home. The stone was then sent to us and set right here and made by hand in their small local workshop. It was so wonderful to sit with their designer Colleen, and sketch what was in my mind. She even suggested adding in Lee's birth stone—peridot—hidden under my diamond, which we LOVED! My ring is everything I dreamt it could be and I couldn't recommend their service enough. We also had our wedding bands done with Affinity.

The Decorations

We used a small female-owned business who pride themselves on reducing and reusing. We had edible fruit like coconuts and pineapples to honor Lee's heritage, and they were also eaten later that night! The furniture used was second hand and the girls did a wonderful job of taking decorations from the ceremony to the reception. Flowers were given to the local hospital after our big day. We also made sure to be a plastic-free wedding—no straws or unnecessary throw-away items.

RESOURCE TOOLS

Sandra Henri from Mindfully Wed is an incredible resource and helped Lee and me so much with our special, sustainable day. Her website has a fantastic guide you can get your hands on.

Everything you will see here is ethical, mindful, sustainable, and aimed at showing you that slowing down never has to mean sacrificing style for your special day, in fact we think it makes it more beautiful! Check out Sandra's amazing checklist below; it's a great tool to help you develop a 'Saying Yes For Less' mindset!

GET CURIOUS

In the words of Sandra Henri, lessstuffmoremeaning.org

Mindful wedding planning and a curious mind are great friends. Reducing a wedding's footprint begins with a state of mind: a willingness to ask questions, and the creativity and courage to go your own way. Here are a few questions to get you started on your journey of wedding rebelliousness. 😉

Where was this made, and was it made fairly? Don't be afraid to ask your dressmaker, jeweler or florist these questions. The reason for this is that wedding suppliers are generally small, service-based businesses who aim to please. More than likely you'll be welcomed with an open mind and "let's find out" approach.

Does it have to be new? There are many ways in which you can integrate the old with the new. Sentimental family jewelry can be recreated into new bespoke pieces, and vintage or dead-stock fabrics to design new gowns. Borrow items where you can; people love to help and contribute to weddings!

How can we reduce waste? Explore re-gifting the flowers following the wedding day or use potted plants instead of florals, ask about nose-to-tail catering where no part is wasted, ask your venue if they recycle or compost, use e-invites and bamboo disposables, or give your bridal party the freedom to wear whatever they want and are likely to wear again.

How can we benefit our local community? Try to source local, organic and support the little guy. There are so many part-time wedding businesses that do a little happy dance every time they get a booking!

How far has this travelled? Give your florist the creativity to use what's in season and grown locally, support a local dressmaker, or choose garden-to-plate catering. Alternatively, if purchasing from overseas, support a traditional artisan, helping to provide employment and preserve culture.

Do we really need this? Set free one layer of your wedding and donate the savings to a cause instead. Or invest in relationship nurturing and coaching that will far outlast any material items on your wedding day.

How can we carbon-offset our wedding or honeymoon? While you might like to get hands-on with tree planting or making a donation, you'll be surprised that the easiest way to carbon-offset your wedding is by increasing the plant-based servings in your wedding menu. You even might save a few dollars while you're at it!

Natural Dyeing with Brown Skin Onions

Mother Nature has always been our greatest muse, effortlessly creating incredible color like it *ain't* no thing.

Sadly though, we humans have strayed from her simplicity. There was a time when natural dyeing was the norm, with no end to what the flower, plant, vegetable and even insect world could whip up. Locally grown, readily available and completely organic was the name of the dyeing game and it's one that dates back more than 5000 years. In this time there was no such thing as synthetic, everything was gloriously slow and done by hand. Cue the mid-19th-century industrial revolution and our disconnect. Suddenly, polyester was propelled into the spotlight and of course we 'needed' synthetic dyes full of dangerous chemicals to service the demand. A time-old tradition was tossed aside. So it was with much interest when I discovered brown onion skin dye while searching for a specific color I wanted for my bridesmaids gowns. Thank you **@fragmentario**. It took me back to my childhood and I was reminded of my mum doing all manner of things with tea, coffee, leaves and flowers to transform her garments. I was hooked! Now I'm no expert but I've certainly been having a ton of fun experimenting, so I thought I'd share how to do it.

Brown Onion Skin Dyeing Method

1. Ask your local grocer to collect brown onion skins for you; seriously they thought I was a little strange at first but when I showed them what I wanted to do they were fascinated and glad to help! You don't need a lot, just a good couple of handfuls will do.
2. Select the item you would like to dye and make sure it's a natural fiber—silk, linen or organic cotton. Give it a good rinse under the tap, wring it out then set it aside.
3. Fill a large pot with water and turn the stove on to get it bubbling away.
4. Once boiling turn it right down and add the onion skins. You'll see the color of the water change pretty quickly to a deep burgundy. Let them simmer in the pot for about an hour, stirring occasionally.
5. Remove the skins with tongs, or if you prefer, pour the dye through a strainer to separate them. I added them to another pot to cool down and then they went in my bokashi bin for composting.
6. Keep it on the simmer and add your garment! The color takes right away, so if you want it on the lighter side submerge it for around 20 mins/half an hour. If you want a deeper shade, leave it for a few hours or even overnight.
7. Rinse it until the water runs clear and hang it out to dry. The sun will set it. Each time you do it, it will be a slightly different tone depending on time, strength and, in my case on this round, a few ring-ins! The result from this batch actually had a few red onion skins sneak in, but I was keen to see what happened. It ended up being a more mustardy tone.

The first time I did it, it was just the brown onion skins and that produces more of a peachy hue. I love them both and also love that you never really know how it will turn out. Half the fun is in the surprise. You can reuse the dye for other items or if you are done, simply share it with your garden, it's all natural so won't hurt a thing.

The color can fade over time, but I just dye it again. I think you can use a mordant like vinegar to set it, but I haven't bothered.

Give it a try, it's so much fun!

Another one to explore is dyeing with avocados and guess what!? It's not the skin but the seed that holds a stunning dusty-pink color. Seriously, Mother Nature is so sublime.

CHAPTER NINE

The Wardrobe Workout

> 'The wardrobe workout is the only type of workout I'll do willingly.'
>
> Amelia @stylestorytellernz

What began as a simple musing in Oct 2019 for me to get more out of my closet has birthed into a beautiful expression of community, inclusivity and eco-chic.

The **#wardrobeworkout** is a regular style challenge on my Instagram **@fayedelanty** based around the concept of finding fabulous new ways to wear your 'old gear.' **#usewhatyouhave**

I encourage dress-up and play time. John Galliano also believes in the power of dress-up days, holding them frequently in his atelier at Maison Margiela to foster creativity, innovation and new ways to cut and remaster clothing, fabric and form.

> 'You need to know the fundamentals first, you can't build the house without the structure and what better way than to try clothes on, try them on inside out, pull them apart, deconstruct them, rebuild them. It's a very real way of learning and experiencing.'
>
> John Galliano

The Wardrobe Workout (WW) was originally just for me to further educate myself in the ways of reducing, reusing and recycling my clothes. To walk my own sustainability talk. But I quickly realized my community was super keen for it too. So, I opened the concept to a special guest each and every session and it's paved the way for the most profound stories to come forward. It's been an amazing ride thus far. I have made incredible friends, and despite the fact many of us have never actually met in person, I am so inspired by their creativity and conscious hearts. Quite a few of my wardrobe workout guests are modelling throughout these pages. Opshopulence is, without a doubt, a love letter to my thrift community too.

Over the last year I have had wardrobe workout co-hosts from all over the world including: New York, The Netherlands, Chicago, Canada, South Africa, Portugal, Nashville and New Zealand. To name but a few.

Even my dad has joined me. I truly see fashion as a powerful vehicle for transformation so I have strategically encouraged my guests to generate a theme with me that not only is a piece of their soul but will tell an inspiring and important story through style.

I am so proud of the topics we have explored to date, which range from:

- self-love
- gender expression
- culture and subcultures like punk, Dandyism and retro futurism
- race and civil rights
- badass modest fashion
- COVID and how the pandemic has affected us as a fashion collective
- inclusivity and diversity

- sexuality
- art
- music
- couture
- color therapy

It's a deep dive into fashion history and how style is always a talisman for what is rumbling among the collective. Through our closets, my community and I have been able to shape-shift.

Reigniting our love for what's languishing in our wardrobes and reimagining how we view the world around us, through the lens of style. There are so many incredible expressions of the WW; to select the stand outs is like picking a favorite fashion child. However, what I will do is highlight the ones that really opened minds and hearts to the max among my gorgeous community.

Jess @the.thrifted.gay

DANDYISM AND ANDROGYNY

Jess @the.thrifted.gay

'Something Faye and I really vibed about together was my love for androgyny. Obviously if you look at me, I'm not your stereotypical 'feminine' woman and I see myself as more androgynous, which means that I'm not masculine, I'm not feminine but I am everything in between.

I kind of always knew I was gay; I just never was ok with that myself. I would constantly tell myself I can't feel this way, it's not what I'm supposed to be feeling. I'm supposed to like boys. I would do anything possible to avoid this feeling. It turned into self-hate. I didn't like the person I was. I didn't like how I felt in my own body. How could I show other people who I really was when I wasn't ok with me being me? The first time I came out was to one of my family members who was super supportive, and I'm very fortunate for that.

From there I gained my confidence.

> Being 'out' helped me discover that loving my style and the person I want to be is so much easier to work towards because I'm accepting every part of the way I am.

I really found my style through the queer community; I had a diversity and inclusion director come up to me in college and say, 'hey, there's a conference coming up, you should come.

I was hesitant at first; I'd never been around so many queer people all at once and I just didn't know if I would fit in. I wasn't masculine presenting then. I had long hair and I would just wrap it up in a bun because I hated it so much. I would wear sweats all the time and I just didn't like what I saw in the mirror. For that director to ask me to come along, it felt so good to know that someone saw me for me.

It's where I learnt about masculine-presenting individuals and how to incorporate that style into every-day life, and from there I just gutted my entire closet. Anything that wasn't me, that I didn't love, I just donated it or gifted to friends and family members. Then I started thrifting, thrifting all the clothes that I wanted to be in, I wanted to look good in. I slowly learnt that it's ok to look this way, to be more masculine. My advice to anyone who's wanting to come out is to just know that it's going to be ok and that you are loved. And when you are ready to come out, we are here to support you in any way. I hope me sharing this story helps someone.

Everyone's coming-out story is worth telling.

> Harry Styles always has a great mix of masculine and feminine looks into one style. A lot of the inspiration for this outfit came from his mix of suits with feminine pieces. I absolutely loved his photo shoot with *Vogue*. It was the perfect androgynous look! He wore skirts with jackets, a button-up with a long coat and blended these very masculine/feminine pieces into one. Inspired by this shoot, I combined a pink-collar button-up with a turtleneck underneath a feminine, sheer, black floral embroidered long shirt. I wanted to give the illusion of wearing a dress (which Harry is known for mixing). For the cherry on top of the femininity touch, I wore pearls. To add a more masculine/edgy look, I wore black combat boots, black slacks and a long black overcoat.

Growing up in a binary world always felt uncomfortable. I never felt completely feminine or masculine. I used to hate what I looked like and never took pictures or was proud of what I saw in the mirror. Thrifting gave me a chance to start over. To really become the person I've always wanted to see in the mirror. It took a ton of trial and error to completely redo my entire wardrobe and find pieces I felt like myself in, rather than looking for the validation of others on what I should be wearing. I never truly was myself until I started to completely thrift.

> In a way, thrifting gave me life.'
>
> Jess @the.thrifted.gay

BUFFALO STANCE

'I don't work out but when it comes to fashion or anything to do with fashion, we can definitely work out anything all day, every day.'

Matthew Fischer @so_fisch

'Faye describes the Wardrobe Workout as something to invoke thought, talk about fashion history, and to embrace creativity through fashion. All clothing, all styles, prints and silhouettes are inspired by something, so we have to embrace these things because isn't it kind of amazing that something as simple as a cerulean sweater (as per *The Devil Wears Prada*) can be traced back to where that color comes from, the influence it has. Buffalo style is a movement of style from West London promoted by the youth culture of never fitting in, punk attitude, self-expression, the idea of friendship and the fearless creative spirit. The name came from the Bob Marley song *Buffalo Soldier*, which was based on the African regiment of the U.S. Army, named by the Native Americans during the Civil War. It referred to how fierce they were. It was pushed forward by stylist Ray Petrie.

When we talk about the Buffalo-boy look, we talk about how it changes gender norms and stereotypes. It brings in ceremonial attire and if anyone knows me, I love ceremonial attire. Royal attire plays a huge part in my look—Princess Diana is one of my all time fave fashion influences. Ray Petrie and his Buffalo gang were a bunch of immigrant families of mixed cultures, mixed races (like me) that pushed the boundaries of what fashion is. These masculine men were wearing skirts, women were wearing suits, underwear became outer wear, and it's the idea of self-expression through fashion. This is definitely something I resonate with every day, especially because I am mixed culture. I am pushing gender norms and stereotypes. I'm from the islands of Hawaii, their mixed culture is such a normal thing that when I moved to the continental U.S., it was definitely an eye-opener to what boxes people try to put you into. They can never figure out what I am, which really shouldn't matter.

But it does.'

CRUELLA DE *THRIFT*-VILLE

As told by Ameila @stylestorytellernz

There are so many things I love about Faye and her "Wardrobe Workout". Not only does she encourage us to look at clothes we already own in a whole new way, but she also provides a great opportunity for escape and distraction from day-to-day challenges in a world that has completely changed in the last two years. The themes Faye sets for herself, and her guests are often educational and always fantastic Cruella de Thrift Ville was perhaps the most fantastical of them all.

Using her powers of persuasion in the best way, Faye convinced me to watch Disney's Cruella. Looking back, it's hard to believe I needed convincing. I watched it repeatedly and an abundance of fashion inspiration hit me like a Jasper driven truck. Which brings me to one scene where Cruella donned a dress made of "trash" in an amazing act of rebellion. It stuck with me, waking me up four nights in a row—ideas on how to recreate it running through my head.

Armed with pieces of chiffon and mesh, pages of magazines and clothes I had put in rubbish bags ready to donate, I folded, buttoned, tied, twisted, and tucked my way to this finished creation. In true Cruella style, I was ready to "make a statement" and there's nothing stopping you from doing the same.

> 'I was born brilliant. Born bad. And a little bit mad.'
>
> Cruella de Ville

'I had no idea where I was or what it was. I just knew that for the first time in my life, I felt like I belonged.'

Cruella de Ville

My covid lockdown cruella creation at home

DAPPER DAN, BLACK LIVES MATTER

Joy @joyebenspiff

Fashion is generalised, style is personalised.

Style is what you make of it. It is a true expression on one's self, expressive enough to say much without speaking, because the clothes speak for themselves.

Wardrobe workout, a term nicely couched by Faye, is a perfect example of building a personal style that was present but dormant. It's a way of pushing your boundaries as to what you think is your style, into what becomes an endless curation of style.

When I worked with Faye highlighting Dapper Dan as our muse, it gave me an opportunity to dig deep into his personality, his journey as a style icon and how fabrics mean a lot to him. I began to understand his craftsmanship, his thought process into every design and detail. It was a true depiction that style doesn't have to be expensive, you just have to have the eye and the taste and it will spring up. I took to his abilities and ran with them, creating a look that portrays who he is and what his designs are made of.

As a black woman living in the United States, it was important for me to highlight something that resonates with the black community. Having witnessed and felt the societal pressure during the Black Lives Matter Movement, I was determined to express myself even more as a black fashionable lady. This helped me understand Dapper Dan, a black man who fought against all odds to get to where he is today.

May we continue to see our clothes past the idea that they are just fabrics, but pieces which embody a spirit that lives on because our clothes are who we truly are.

@joyebenspiff

Top 10 Wardrobe Workout Tips

1. Behold... the belt

They cinch us in, create detail for jackets and dresses, and bring that designer drama. I always look in the men's section of thrift stores for vintage leather belts. The longer length allows me to use my favorite looping trick à la McQueen and Vivienne Westwood for a high fashion finish.

Head to **opshopulence.com** for the demo.

2. Play with proportions

Try:

- A crop-top over a silk blouse or button-down
- A dress over pants. If it's too long, hike it up and tuck in one side for interesting asymmetry
- Leather and lace, a tee with tailoring, sequins in the day time
- Don't be afraid to experiment with your style. Trust me, you'll see it on the runways! Check out Vogue Runway for incredible inspiration from all the shows

3. Couture-*ify* your classics

Simple switches and divine details can make all the difference towards a designer feel.

- Switch out boring plastic buttons for brass, gold, or silver military ones
- Wear a corset-style top over a simple button-down shirt or a t-shirt, add a lightweight blazer

@shaqaeqrezai

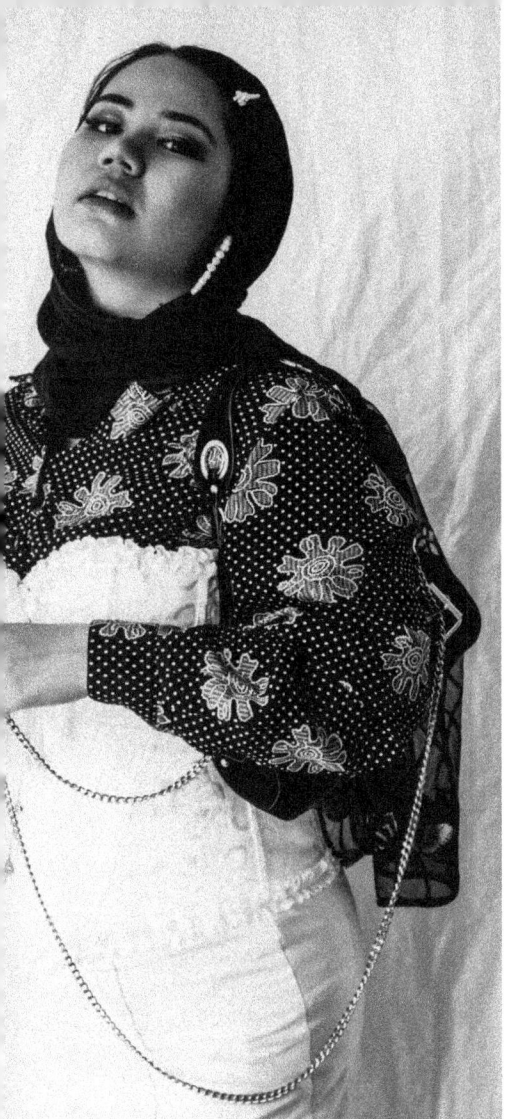

- Layer necklaces
- Try oversized pieces for an expensive aesthetic; pushing up the sleeves, cinching in the waist and popping the collar can look a million bucks
- Be drawn to natural fibers as much as possible—linen, silk, wool, cotton, and leather all have a luxe appeal

4. Flip it and reverse it

Be open to bold new ideas for old friends. Try wearing your blouses backwards, flip your collar.

Could a long skirt be a dress, or an oversized shirt a skirt? You never know what's possible until you try.

@emilykatesymes in my reversed men's shirt creation

5. Get ye some 'fash-ed'

Study fashion history. Explore different eras, styles, designers, subcultures and genres. This is how my **#wardrobeworkout** series started. I wanted to get more out of my closet, and I realized that I didn't need more clothes; I just needed to exercise my inner fashion designer. Expanding my knowledge was the key, and an incredible catalyst for creativity.

6. The wise customize

One of my favorite things to do is to *crop it while it's hot.* I snip the bottom of too-long or outdated jeans. Slice an oversized button-down to create a cool new look. I crop trench coats, and add extra layers to skirts with scarves and material. To seal the deal, I throw cropped pieces in the washing machine to encourage that rough-hem edge.

7. Shop and swap

I love raiding my husband's wardrobe and exchanging items with friends. It's a wonderful way to put together *new to me* looks. It feels fresh without having to spend a cent. Renting from a store like EKOLUV is another great option to try 'new' styles and keep our style circular. Also check out **@the_swapchain** on Instagram—you'll meet the creator Patrick Duffy in Chapter 13.

8. Accessories bring the A-game

I collect brooches for embellishment... on everything. I collect scarves too, and turn them into tops, asymmetrical panels and designer-inspired handles on bags. Earrings, beautiful fine-gold chains and, of course, a bright red lip take your pieces to the next level.

9. Have a dressmaker on speed dial

I've said it once, I'll say it again: *game changer.* Get your pieces altered and tailored to fit you perfectly. Have missing buttons, loose hems and holes mended or, even better, learn to do that for yourself. I also work with my dressmaker to reimagine tired pieces with a fresh fit.

10. Always apply the finer details

- French cuff your sleeves *(See opshopulence.com for the demo)*
- Get yourself some sleeve garters to keep jackets up
- Keep your shoes clean and mended if needed
- Add accents to your look that show who you are. For me, it's brooches or a bold red lip
- Build your foundational pieces and classic items (like a black dress, great blazer, shirt dress, good-quality denim and tees) first, then add quirk and personality from there
- Make your wardrobe shop-able and be sure the pieces are right for your lifestyle. I do this by color-coding, making it seasonal (when its summer, I put heavy winter items away)
- Use wooden hangers, have helpful storage solutions
- Declutter on the regular and make sure every item is being loved, worn and truly appreciated. If it isn't donate, recycle or sell.

A conscious closet creates space for your true style to emerge. Give your wardrobe a workout and be sure it works hard for you!

For more tips and tricks, follow me on Instagram: **@fayedelanty**

CHAPTER TEN

The Charity Shop Challenge

My beautiful Aunty Zena

The Charity Shop Challenge came about while living in my hometown of Surrey, England, with my Aunty Zena.

Aunty is a charity shop queen and can find the most incredible pieces for minimum spend. It's where she uncovers the majority of the amazing vintage and antique jewelry she sells online and at fairs. Chauffeured by our trusty stead—aka Uncle Ian—Aunty and I would pick a little British town in our county and hunt around their second hand stores, such as Save the Children, RSPCA, Sue Ryder, Salvation Army... whatever we could spy!

With a budget of 5-10 quid, we would get our thrift on and look for what would be a welcome addition to our wardrobes or collection. I coined these thrift-ventures 'The Charity Shop Challenge' (charity shopping is what the Brits call thrifting/op-shopping), and not only did we have an absolute ball, Aunty gave me an invaluable education. I truly believe it's played a big part in the work I'm honored to do today. So here's my gift of thrift to you: behold The Charity Shop Challenge...

In three easy expressions, pick your level and play along.

ONE DAY

For the virgin thrifter

Today you will challenge yourself to take a walk on the wildly slow side, step away from the high-street and simply stroll into a second hand store instead.

Do a quick Google search to determine the locations in your area and decide to which thrift store you are going to head.

Before you go, write a little list of three things you'd like to add or need in your wardrobe.

Challenge yourself to look for one thing in your local thrift store from that list. Perhaps you need a new blazer? Or you love rock tees? Just pick one thing and look only for that.

If you can't find the first thing you were after, go to number two or three on your list.

Or my tip? Head to the accessories section and select something you like. Maybe it's a vintage brooch, a fantastic leather belt or a beautiful scarf.

Start simply and stay open to the experience. How could you style your first thrift find with your existing wardrobe? Have fun experimenting!

Journal some Opshopulence musings
—what did you find, how did you feel on the One Day challenge?

ONE WEEK

For the fledging eco-thriftanista

So you've dabbled and have a few pieces already from a thrift store and you're ready to spread your sustainability wings—wonderful!

For this one-week challenge, I encourage you to create a runway or street-style inspired look using some of your existing thrift pieces, and to go hunting for the rest in your local thrift store to complete the outfit.

Step 1. Choose the look you are lusting after. Check out Vogue Runway, it's got all the shows, designer reviews and street-style. Alternatively, just scroll through a magazine or social media. Pinterest or Instagram are goldmines.

Step 2. Work out what you already have in your wardrobe that could be reworked to recreate this look. Perhaps it's a pencil skirt or a white tee, lay them out on the bed and start to brainstorm.

Step 3. Head to your local thrift store for the rest. Take your inspo pic and hunt only for items that fit the feel. Start to open your mind to the possibilities of restyling. Could a scarf be worn in a stylish or unexpected way?

Perhaps you might like to try your hand at some simple DIY—like pinning a brooch on a clutch bag to give it designer-bling feels—to recreate what you see in your inspo outfit.

Step 4. Document this momentous occasion! Share the story, snap a pic, inspire others to do the same! Tag me on Insta **#opshopulence**

Pencil in your musings and discoveries from the One Week challenge

ONE MONTH

You're going pre-loved profesh

For the One Month Charity Shop Challenge, I set you the task of one designer-inspired look every week for four weeks.

Follow the same guidelines as the One Week challenge.

You've done it once, you know you can do it again and again.

Pencil in your One Month musings

....

....

....

BONUS ROUND

Check out the $2 or clearance rack in your local thrift store and see what you could put together from items hanging here.

Honestly, every time I look on these racks, I find something I could restyle.

If you're feeling really bold, try a whole outfit.

Or, if you want to take it at a snail's pace perhaps just one item that you could add to an existing look to mix it up.

You don't have to buy it either, it could just be a mini Charity Shop Challenge in-situ.

Remember, op shops allow you to play, so dive into a dress-up sesh.

Chances are you'll convince yourself and it will come home with you but remember, sustainable style first and foremost—if you don't truly love or need it, leave it for someone else.

ONE LOVE

One love is when you've decided to break-up with fast-fashion for good because you've fallen in love with the slow lane.

Seriously, congratulations.

I don't blame you. I mean, how good is it? You've gone from challenge to a lifestyle choice, a decision to put the planet first and I couldn't be more proud.

Go forth and be pre-loved pretty!

Keep the concept of my charity shop adventures with Aunty close to your heart and inspire others to do the same.

Revive Festival 2019. All models styled by yours truly using absolutely everything second hand from @salvostores

CHAPTER ELEVEN

The Opshopulent Man

MY HUSBAND'S STYLE REINVENTION

While I never set out to intentionally change Lee's look, over the years of doing what I do, my divine husband started paying more attention and asking questions. Lee is a spiritual man, and he could see the type of fashion I work with seems to have a profound effect on a lot of people I come into contact with. It sparked his curiosity. 'Could you dress me, babe', he asked one day, and let's be honest—you don't have to do that twice! So we began to explore a wardrobe reinvention together. The more I came to understand his soul, the more I could see how I could help Lee bring that out through his clothing choices, in turn really expressing the beautiful and unique individual he is. Never preaching or pushing, always empowering him to make the style moves. As a duo we've discovered so many great style tricks, so here's a few to help the lads in your life on their way to Opshopulence.

FIVE STYLE LESSONS FROM LEE

1. Start with the basics in classic neutral shades

- A crisp white button-down
- Good quality black and blue jeans in modern, flattering cuts
- A fresh white tee
- A tailored suit
- Classic cargo pants or chinos

These are the canvas pieces upon which you can build individual character and quirk.

2. Muse on the elements that make you, you

Lee loves: crystals, feathers, Native American culture, Elvis, the cowboy aesthetic, Bruce Lee and throwbacks to the 30s and 40s speakeasies.

So we've developed ways to add these accents to complement his canvas pieces. This is how we bring out the essence of the man Lee is, what's in his heart and his fashion DNA. We've found him some fantastic vintage cowboy boots, all thrifted, and invested in beautiful Australian-made Akubra hats, to which we add feathers, a masculine hat pin or brooch to suit his outfit accordingly.

I'm sure to look for moments where I can celebrate Lee's heritage through his outfit choices. Born in Tonga, my husband has beautiful brown skin and traditional Pacific Islander tattoos that tell the story of his ancestors. So a simple French cuff on a button-down, or rolled-up sleeves on a vintage tee, show a peak of his Polynesian roots, which he is rightly so very proud of.

3. Accessories A-game

They are devoid of size or age and an incredible way to show the world who you are. Each one of Lee's sterling silver rings tells a story and kinda gives him a spiritual Karl Lagerfeld vibe, which I love.

4. Divine details

If jewelry isn't your thing, there are so many other ways to express your style via accessories—the power is in the details. Explore cravats, pocket squares, a chic pair of glasses, a beautiful timepiece, silk ties, scarves, or even a sharp haircut can tell your style story. Personalizing, customizing and monogramming accessories is another great trick. I source Lee classic vintage leather belts, then have them embossed with his initials for a special touch. *Fun fact:* If you noticed the G on his belt, Lee's full first name is actually Gottliep which means 'God's Love'. Lee is an abbreviation and ode to his idol, Bruce Lee.

5. Pinterest

Just like I do for myself, I create mood boards on Pinterest for my husband too. Then I sit with him and we muse together. I love hearing his take and ideas; he teaches me a lot. These are boards we can come back to time and again to update or be inspired by looks we may have missed before. This is a great way to make the most of what you already have. I really enjoy empowering Lee to make style choices that feel right for him.

While Lee looks fantastic, I think what fills me with even more joy is seeing how Lee struts into a room and really owns it these days. I've watched how the right clothes have increased his confidence, illustrating to me yet again the power style can have to change our state. I love the power it can create for us as a couple too. The way Lee and I dress when we go places together has been incredible for sparking conversations. More often than not, people will notice our pre-loved details and make comment or ask questions. When we tell them it's all thrifted, ethical and second hand they 100% of the time want to know more. I'm so proud that we can ignite important sustainability conversations through style. What's even cooler is that we've thrifted 90% of it, adding in ethically-made items like his Akubra hats to seal the sustainable man deal.

One evening on our couch with cups of tea in hand, I mused with my amazing hubby on his style evolution. Here's what transpired.

Faye: How would you describe your style now, and your style before you met me?

Lee: Before I met you, normal Bruce Lee t-shirt, pair of jeans, converse... I used to wear a lot of bold colors because I work with elements, colors, chakras... being Islander, I love colors but I didn't know how to make it work like I do now. I overdid it. In contrast, I used to wear a lot of black because of my job. This black started to blend into my other days. Mostly just black jeans and black t-shirt or Bruce Lee tee. Style wasn't a huge focus for me, I just grabbed stuff. Only if I went out would I think about my look. Whatever felt easy and quick and was clean.

Now, you've changed my perception of style. I see details, I see meaning. You've made me more stylish. You've pimped my ride!

How does it make me feel? More confident, like I can own the room. I love the cravats and different trimmings you've shown me how to add—you shape-shift, babe. Your sister's wedding was the first time I wore a cravat, and you gave me your Hermès scarf to try. I feel like I really channeled

> 'Absorb what is *useful*, reject what is useless, add what is essentially your own."
>
> - Bruce Lee

the Hermes energy (Hermes is one of the most intelligent and mischievous of the Greek gods. He symbolizes wealth, luck and fertility). It was pretty cool how at the wedding so many people wanted to know about my outfit. I love that I now see how clothes help me embody different elements of my soul. I love that I can shape-shift through my style, spark conversations, people look at you differently and that feels good.

What we wear has a meaning. It feels right doing the right thing and that affects how you feel about yourself. I am an old soul, have had many lifetimes—German, Polynesian, Portegeuse. I feel them and it's wonderful that I can honor them through what I wear and how I express myself.

Faye: How do you feel about your wardrobe now?

Lee: It's full of surprises and meaning, full of different lifetimes. It's a bag of tricks! I like that you come home with gifts for me. It's a collaboration and really fun to see it all come together. I get the wardrobe workout everyday; I'm a lucky guy!

Faye: What are your fave pieces?

Lee: Cravats, hats, brooches—especially our Scottish sword/kilt pin. It's a great conversation starter and helps me embrace the guardian protector knighthood energy I feel drawn to. I always feel like I have something to wear, and I see what you mean about the canvas pieces now—they make a lot of sense. I take more risks now because of you.

Faye: What made you trust me to embark on this style reinvention together?

Lee: I just felt open to it, ready for it because you were so gentle about it. I knew something good would come of it because I could see the effect you were having on others. And to help guys wake up. I wanted to represent the male side of things. Encourage guys to thrift, show them why it's so powerful and purpose driven. I feel so confident to op shop now.

Faye: How would you describe my style?

Lee: Your style is many and varied! Very McQueen/Westwood! Multi-dimensional. Diverse. I like that you absorb and adapt. I've seen your style evolve; it's become deeper, richer, more detailed. I love your style and how much thought and pride you put into it, which I know comes from your dad too. It's definitely rubbed off on me.

Faye: How do the outfits we create for you together, make you feel?

Lee: Happy, confident, cool, stylish, elevated, meaningful, fun! We have lots of fun!

Faye: Do you believe our clothes can be transformational?

Lee: Yep, for sure. I truly believe that. I see how it affects people around us, our style really draws them in to something more meaningful. It's so much more than just a piece of cloth; it carries an energy... you bring it to life.

Faye: What advice would you give to other men who might want to tap into their Opshopulence?

Lee: Be open, learn the history of style, apply it. Knowledge is not enough, you must do it. I would ask them what they like, get their personal needs, their lifestyle, and go from there. Find something or someone they look up to, a style idol, dress up like them, be it an actor, singer, sportsman... emulate their style and you'll start to develop yours.

FIFTH DIMENSIONAL FASHION

Another element of Lee's style which has inspired me a lot is his love of colors. Together we have found ways to implement them as stylish accents and talking points in his outfits and mine. There are seven special colors in particular Lee would love me to mention. These colors are connected to the Chakra system of your body. These are your energy points right down your center.

Crown—*white*
Third eye—*indigo*
Throat—*blue*
Heart—*pink and green*
Belly—*power center yellow*
Sacral—*orange*
Root—*red fire*

There is an essence to each color and you can use them to amplify and empower that aspect of yourself by strategically choosing them in the clothes you wear.

White: purity, ascension, takes you to a higher place, clarity, blank canvas, uplifting.

Faye's styling tip: I adore white, and personally love it head to toe. So crisp, so fresh. To make it interesting, play with textures and contrasting fabrics such as leather, lace, wool, cotton, patent. Mix and match. Or for everyday—and if coffee or red wine might be present—try just a dash of white with a bag, a white shoe or t-shirt, even just earrings or a brooch.

Indigo/purple: transformation, higher love, compassion, forgiveness, transmuting negative to positive and into freedom.

Faye's styling tip: I personally don't wear this color but I adore it on others. My approach would be a pop paired back with a neutral. I think purple looks incredible with beige and caramel tones. Try a mauve sweater with beige pants, or a beautiful purple silk scarf with a trench coat.

Blue: communication, protection, faith, courage, divine masculine power, stepping into your power. Speak your truth, optimism, focus.

Faye's styling tip: For me it's faded vintage denim all the way! A great lived-in and loved cropped denim jacket with a classic black pleated skirt and boots. Lee looks amazing in his vintage Levi shirt with pearl buttons teamed with a cravat and chinos. Electric blue can be incredibly striking too, especially in silk!

Pink: divine love, kindness, feminine, self-love and one love.

Faye's styling tip: I used to live in this shade when I was little girl so I think I OD'd but I've been implementing dashes of it lately especially with my love of natural dyeing. I would team this with neutrals and crisp whites, it would also look fantastic with khaki green.

Green: healing, abundance, manifestation from your heart, new growth, earth energy, you rep for Mother Earth when you wear this color—bringing awareness to her healing through your clothes.

Faye's styling tip: Khaki and army fatigues is my fave shade of green. I'd happily wear it head to toe, but also love pops of neon green or mint green, which look fantastic with creamy, coffee, caramel tones. Apply liberally.

Yellow: wisdom, divine mind, power center, thinking Opshopulent thoughts in this hue for the highest good, illumination like the sun.

'Let the sun shine in'—The 5th Dimension, 1969

The sun empowers and gives life, where we draw our energy from, happiness.

Faye's styling tip: I think head to toe yellow looks incredible, you can't help but feel happy but if this too much for you, try a flowy skirt and white t-shirt, a vintage silk blazer or even a shoe. I have a great pair of pointy-toe patent kitten heels that look wonderful with simple denim and a basic t-shirt.

Orange: co-creativity and what you bring to the table, sexual/creative energy, bring life either in physical or spirituality/evolutionary sense. Resurrection—how we reuse and remaster our Opshopulent looks.

Faye's styling tip: I have the most amazing bright orange, vintage pleated skirt. It even has the tulle under skirt, she is such a dream. I thrifted her for $10! I have worn this beauty so many times. My tip here is to let this color pop and keep everything else simple. I personally love it with a contrasting black jacket and boots but have also worn it with similar tones—an orange tie-dyed tee, leopard coat and cream lace-up boots. Orange tones can even look amazing in eyeshadows or lipsticks. Or a shoe or bag! Even a bangle. I think the great thing about implementing these colors is that there are so many simple and subtle ways to do it. Even the smallest nod activates the elements for me.

Red: passion, fire, what drives you, ambition, confidence, put your stamp on things. Style with a wax seal!

Faye's styling tip: I adore a red suit jacket with a simple white tee and jeans or black pants. I'm also a huge fan of a red lip—so simple but it really elevates an outfit. Could also be highlighted in a vintage silk scarf or a fire-engine red stiletto or converse high top!

The whole mission here is to find ways that colors work for you and have fun. Play around with our ideas or develop your own. One thing is for sure, it will *color you happy* and elevate your everyday.

RE-FASHION WEEK, NYC FEBRUARY 2020

Hosted by donateNYC and the Sanitation Foundation, Refashion Week NYC spotlights second hand and sustainable fashion across New York City with a series of events designed to reimagine the fashion industry from head to toe. From clothing repair workshops to thrift markets to runway shows, it brings New Yorkers together to build a world where style and sustainability go hand in hand.

Here's why Refashion Week is vital. The average NYC household throws away about 120 pounds of textiles a year! And that doesn't even include waste generated from the fashion industry.

Approximately 200,000 tons of clothing, shoes, linens, and accessories are sent to landfill every year! New York City's annual textile waste is equivalent to:

- Nearly 900 Statues of Liberty
- Over 4,500 subway cars
- 13.5 Brooklyn Bridges

We can make a difference. By keeping 200,000 tons of textiles a year out of landfills, we can reduce greenhouse gas emissions by 1,231,917 metric tons, and energy usage by 9,707,680 million BTUs! That is the equivalent of:

- Planting 378,338 acres of air-cleaning forests
- Keeping 266,073 cars off the road for one year

2020's Refashion Week had over 4000 attendees across 20+ events and resulted in 2.5 tons of clothing swapped, mended, or otherwise rescued from landfill.

> 'I believe that refashion week is the world's hope for a brighter future. Our planet depends on innovative brands problem solving in a collaborative manner. Embracing second hand fashion and upcycling unwanted items is of great value.'
>
> @rosiemae27

@mrpatrickduffy and me at The Empty Shop in NYC

In February 2020 I had the honor of flying to New York and being on the board of Refashion Week—helping to shape the week's happenings, promotion and publicity as well as hosting an event. As a representative for my Salvos Stores colleagues in Australia, and with the help of the amazing Patrick Duffy (who you will meet in the next chapter), we set up the 'Empty Shop' to promote our Moving The Needle (MTN) initiative. MTN is about bringing brands, charity, and the collective together to work on solutions for textile waste.

As its name suggests, The Empty Shop is a shop with absolutely nothing in it. The purpose is to encourage community to bring good quality donations to help us fill it up. Every day the donated clothing was styled and then shipped off to our NYC charity partner, Goodwill. It was also an incredible way to start conversations about circularity and the importance of a more conscious fashion industry. We first tested the idea the year before in Sydney and the publicity for it went viral, so we knew it was the perfect approach to try in NYC!

We hosted a Fashion Revolution panel with other change-makers in the fashion industry and it was so incredibly well received. I even got us on NY1, the news channel all New Yorkers watch. This was in a pre-COVID NYC too, so I hold this memory very dear. As I write this in 2021, I am thrilled to say I am on the board again but sadly just from my lounge room, thanks to international travel restrictions still being in place. We do, however, have some fantastic digital ideas planned.

For the two weeks that Lee and I were in NYC we saw time and time again how our thrifted outfits would ignite conversation. People would literally stop us in the street to find out where things were from or comment how we just looked 'so different' or 'unique': "You guys don't look like everyone else."

And the thrifting there, oh my goodness, so many gems! I was super impressed with how intentional we both were. If it didn't fit in our suitcase, it couldn't come home with us.

Speaking on the Fashion Revolution panel at the Canvas for Refashion Week 2020

We had a special Empty Shop launch party, and I thrifted my entire look from Goodwill for $30. It consisted of:

1. A super oversized 80s faux khaki-green leather bomber jacket for $10. It was huge on me but I knew what I could do. I popped the collar, pushed up the sleeves, cinched the waist with my Moschino belt and encrusted the lapel with brooches. It looked amazing.
2. I teamed it with a nude, pleated midi skirt that cost $5.
3. Nude lace-up mid-rise heeled boots for $15. They were the absolute perfect match of nude shade so they just morphed into each other and really let the jacket pop. Plus, they made me look long—gotta love that when you're 5'4.

Guests asked me all night about my ensemble, and I felt so proud to tell them the origin and to share all my thrifty restyling tips, and many of the girls said they were off thrifting the next day! To me that is the best compliment ever.

I feel like so much of this book was sparked from that trip; it had such a transformational effect on both of our style, and we grew to value its message even more. We could feel the very tangible shift in the NYC-mindset around purposed-driven clothing. I swear you could cut the air with it. It was absolutely incredible to be a part of Refashion Week, to see the ethical designer talent in the city, the way New Yorkers are viewing second hand and we can't wait to be back rocking our thrift in the city.

Big, beautiful, sustainable things are brewing.

Lee and I at the Refashion Week Change-Makers dinner, West Village NYC dressed in head to toe thrift

CHAPTER TWELVE

Next Gen
Opshopulence

I may not have children of my own, but I do have 32 nieces and nephews on my husband's side, and Lee and I are proud godparents to Miss Vivian via our dear friends Anita and James. It fills me with so much joy to dress these divine little beings, to see them beam with confidence as they swirl and strut in their op shop finery.

Just as there is unlimited potential in thrift stores for us grown-ups, the same goes for the mini-me's in our life. I think it's a really profound lesson to teach them about the merits of pre-loved shopping. To show the next generation that shopping consciously can have a big impact on the world around them.

Kids grow incredibly fast and really are not fussed about fancy brands. So if you ask me, it makes no sense to spend a fortune on clothes they will only wear for a short time. If there's one thing I hope I've shown you, is that absolutely anyone can look first class in second hand chic. Why can't it be the same for our children? I truly believe that if we teach our little ones to take pride in what they wear and give them plenty of opportunities to express who they are through style, it can really foster a fabulous relationship with self, empowering them as they grow into young adults.

Joining me for this chapter are some absolutely fabulous Opshopulent fashionistas—Isabella, Christina and Michael, and their mum Ruth; Paula and her daughter Liya, and Miss Indi Field, a next generation thrift fanatic and really flawless young woman, paving the way for her generation to get their Opshopulence on. Indi has also created all the amazing illustrations in this book.

Here are my thoughts on how to develop an Opshopulent wardrobe for your kids, ages 2 and upwards. This is the approach I take with the little ones in my life.

For the really little ones you can find fantastic quality rompers, onesies and playsuits second hand that will get you through the newborn stage. I also highly recommend checking out Miss Vivian's Mummy, Anita, and her book *A Zero Waste Family*. This tracks Anita's journey into motherhood and how she did it eco-luxe style. Lots of tips and tricks for a zero waste and wonderfully conscious bubba and parents.

5 TIPS FOR OPSHOPULENT KIDS

1. Start with hardy, good quality natural fibers that wash and wear well. These will be the wardrobe staples

Look for:

- Cotton t-shirts and singlets
- Denim—shorts, jeans, skirts
- Linen dresses, shirts, pants
- Cotton leggings

I constantly see high-end kids' brands in thrift stores, especially items like Ralph Lauren, Polo, Tommy Hilfiger, Osh Kosh, Bonds, Marc Jacobs, Calvin Klein, and for the most part these items are in natural fibers.

2. Determine your child's character

- What are their fave colors?
- What are you already noticing about who they are?
- Are they a girly-girl who loves pink or is she more like I was, a total tomboy until I hit 7-8 years of age and was repelled by that shade.
- Is your boy a real rough and tumble or is he more into books and quieter pursuits?
- Where are they showing their creativity?
- How are they presenting? There are so many beautiful expressions, stay open.
- What stories are they drawn to?

All these elements can help you decide together what they might like to wear.

3. Mix and mash it up

I don't see any reason why girls can't wear boy's gear and vice versa, especially when we are talking classic items and neutral tones. When I shop for the little ones in my life, I look in the entire kids' section, not just their gender-specific section. A cool boy's tee can look great on a girl, as can girl's denim items on the boys. Just try and play around; you'll be surprised what's possible.

As I do for the grown-ups, look to Pinterest and create boards for inspo. I also tap into the process intuitively with similar questions and musings to what I have asked you above. The aim is to let who they are shine through and encourage them to be a part of the creative dressing process. I truly feel that my parents doing this for me has without a doubt helped me in my adult life, giving me confidence with how to present myself in my own unique way.

RUTH & HER ECO-CHIC TRIBE

Thrift-stylist, Poshmark reseller, and one of my fave pre-loved angels on the internet. Based in Canada.

Ruth has incredible thrift style and three of the chic-est kiddos you'll ever see, all with very clear visions on how they want to look. So here are Ruth's musings and tips.

Each one of my kids picked their outfits. In my house I give you a bible of principles but it is within you to execute it and develop your style. I don't believe in pushing someone to wear something they do not like. My children are given the freedom to express themselves. What and when they want to wear a piece again, follows simple principles.

Ruth and kids: Isabella (eldest), Christina (the middle one), Michael (youngest)

Isabella is a practical stylist, she knows what she wants to wear and when to wear it. In her book, there are days to be a princess and days to be a tomboy, it all depends on her mood and occasion. In this particular outfit, she resembles what she calls, 'Cool Mom vibes'. The animal print bodysuit paired with a sweet embroidery mini dress, topped up with the cool denim jacket and some timeless Dr. Martens. Isabella is the child I have the most fun with because she's never scared of something new.

Meet Christina, a fashionista and stylist specialized in making you feel fancy no matter the time of the day. Christina will cry and say, 'It's not my style' if I put something on her that is not in the Christina's fancy outfits book. Christina knows what she wants to wear each and every single day and will not let the world mess with that. I admire this child and learn from her each day. She chose the fancy ballerina outfit.

Meet Michael, fashionista in training. Michael is only two and the reason why I say he is in training is only because he doesn't have the principles defined yet. He's still learning them but that doesn't stop him creating his very own outfits, and you can't mess with that. He also chose his look. Michael is all about business and his outfits tell that head to toe.

Developing a sense of conscious style in our little ones all starts in changing your mind for a better world. I believe this land is in the hands of our children (the future) and we have to synchronize and pass our values to our children, the importance of buying second hand, to become independent of fashion trends, to be your own designer, to navigate and develop your own sense of style.

I teach my children to:
- Focus on buying natural fabrics, which mean better quality and longevity
- Stick with what they love
- Not buy anything just because it's cheap
- Ask questions like 'do I really need it?'
- Know that the first step to develop a sense of style (and I say develop because we are all born with it) is to create a small collection of good quality basics like:
  - a crisp button-down
  - white, grey, blue and black jeans
  - a basic t-shirt
  - a graphic tee
  - denim jacket
  - moto jacket
  - flowy dress
  - tulle skirt
  - chambray shirt
  - sneakers and combat boots
  - a pair of ballet flats

These basics will create such stylish outfits and so many options. These are the pieces I have for my children. We also have a very busy household, so the less time we have to spend worrying about what to wear the better, we can look and feel good effortlessly. I love seeing my kids confident in their clothes and themselves. I truly believe thrifting has been such a great and meaningful adventure to take with them.

PAULA & LIYA

'I am educating my daughter Liya to find joy in pre-loved and thrifted fashion. Not only from an environmental standpoint but also not to have any embarrassment about thrifting. Pre-loved fashion is nothing to be embarrassed about; it's actually a source of beautiful fashion and style. It also keeps clothes out of landfill, which is extremely important. Thrifting is something we should all do more of.'

Paula and Liya Mugabi

@mspaulapresents

INDI FIELD

Next-generational thrifter

I've lost many a wonderful hour chatting to this super inspiring young woman. Indi truly is out of this world. Keen thrifter, passionate environmentalist and talented artist, I thought I would share one of our recent musings together.

@thriftwithindi

FDL: Indi, I've known you since were a little bubba. You're a teenager now, so tell me how you were drawn to thrifting? Is it in your DNA?

IF: Funnily enough, it is in my DNA! My beautiful Nan (Maria) volunteered at Salvos for many years, and I would go to work with her to dress up all the mannequins! Ever since I was little I have had a love for things like fashion, shopping, and crafts. There are so many photos of me dressing up. One day it was Cinderella, the next day it was Audrey Hepburn.

My parents are so incredible because they would (and still do) always buy me little craft kits, sewing boxes and more recently, my own sewing machine! So I can make little bags using simple things like felt and wool. Having the ability to sew is the foundation of my second hand addiction, because I know I can make something fit, or make something my own.

Thrifting has always been around me, and it was only recently that I made it a full-time thing (around school). I love how every piece of clothing is individual, and there is something for everyone! People at thrift shops always seem like genuine, kind people and being exposed to these people from a young age provided me with a positive vibe with thrifting and second hand or circular fashion.

FDL: Why do you thrift?

IF: I thrift (mainly) to send out the message that things are not alright in the world, whether it is to support less fortunate people through foundations the thrift shops support, or to do our small bit to reduce our carbon footprint on our beautiful Earth. Hopefully if we do our bit, the future generations can live a safe and healthy life.

After watching documentary after documentary on fast, unethical and unsustainable fashion, I felt a true feeling of disgust, a feeling I had never felt before. I want to do something for the people who work tirelessly, on small wages, for the people who get abused, hurt, and sick in these conditions. I want to help stop child labor overseas, and allow these kids to live their lives to the fullest, not in a sweatshop where their voices are not heard. I want to help save the animals whose homes are being destroyed so humans can wear something once then throw it away, I want to help prepare the Earth for the future generations. We have such a beautiful home that we're destroying, and we need to do something about our bad ways before it's too late.

FDL: You have a fantastic Instagram account **@thriftwithindi** where you post lots of pre-loved inspo. Why are you so passionate about second hand?

IF: Ever since I was little, I've had a burning desire to be different, and to stand out from everyone else. I've never been one to blend in with the crowd. At a second hand shop, not only can I get clothes that no one else has, I can also curate my own style using bits and pieces of other people's closets. I love the stories these clothes carry, and the adventures they have been on. Clothing holds so many memories, especially second hand clothing. Also, nothing beats a second hand bargain!

> I love having so much freedom in a second hand shop, I mean it's millions of people's closets all in one!

What more could I ask for? I honestly think it's an addiction at this point, not to the clothing, but to the thrift store itself. But I love it! I love giving clothing a second chance, and styling them in a new way!

FDL: Do your friends/family thrift? What do they think of you doing it? Are you cool or are you weird/different!?

IF: My friends are constantly asking me to go thrifting with them, and I always get told how cool my looks are! Lots of my friends at school follow my Instagram page, and tell me when they go thrifting, *plus* they show me what they thrifted and how they style their second hand clothes! I also spend significant time with my family, my Aunty Venessa, Nanny (Maria), my cousins and anyone else I can get thrifty with. My aim is to get as many people in my generation to start thrifting, so seeing all these people who are my age, all thrifting and loving to buy second hand because of me is seriously incredible.

When I started my page, I was a bit of an outcast at school. There were always people who thought thrifting was for "poor people." So I copped a bit of resistance for it. But if I have learned anything from my parents, it's to prove the mean people wrong, and to do what I love! I could've stopped thrifting a month after I started, and gave into the resistance, but I remembered that I'm not buying second hand for no reason, I'm buying second hand for the mistreated humans overseas in sweatshops and to help carve a sustainable path for the future, and here I am with all these incredible positive and supportive friends who follow in my (sustainable) footsteps!

FDL: As a young woman, how much pressure do you feel to have the latest, greatest, and newest clothes? Do you see your friends going through that?

IF: Unfortunately, people as young as me feel so much pressure to meet certain standards of not only fashion, but personality. People my age are expected to stay silent and listen to the older generations, but unfortunately if we continue to listen to (some) older generations, future generations will live in a disgusting and polluted world full of mistreatment and unjust behavior.

I personally don't feel pressure (anymore). I realized that people won't find interest in me if I look like everyone else, and not myself. When I had this realization, I started following my heart, this was also when people started to recognize me, and support what I do. I made so many new friends and learned so much about myself. I mean it would be great to have all the latest trends, and all the latest looks, but I love having my own style. I love the freedom I have to be myself and express my style.

Part of my mission is to inspire other young people to find themselves in their style, and wear what makes them feel happy. I love the quote (said by Halima Aden) "How boring would this world be if everyone was the same?" I ask myself this when I am branching out of my comfort zone, it is a reminder that what I am doing with sustainable, ethical and circular fashion is good, and I'm not here to be the same as everyone else, I'm here to be Indi.

FDL: What eco-advice would you give your generation? Do you inspire/guide your parents in the ways of thrifting too?

IF: Wake up and know what you are investing into. Is this the best choice for your future? Starting small by knowing what you are buying, where did it come from, do you compare the price of the fashion to the price the Earth pays?

Sustainable and ethical fashion doesn't have to be boring. A tip that I always follow is to use fashion in a way that expresses how I feel. Everybody deserves to have a voice, but some of us have a hard time finding it. Use fashion as your voice! Use fashion as your billboard. I use fashion as a way to inspire the next generation to choose a more sustainable and ethical path for the generations after us. Also, when you're about to invest in something, ask yourself who is this helping, ask do you truly need it, and if you buy it, who will it affect?

Part of sustainable and eco-fashion is minimizing your closet, and not overloading on things you don't need. Asking yourself these questions can help you cut down on the masses of clothing in your closet, while helping save the environment!

My dad taught me a rule many years ago, "Do you want it, or do you need it?" If you're ever stuck on buying an item, ask yourself this, and you will for sure come to a conclusion.

My parents have definitely been buying second hand more! Mostly because I drag them along on my thrift trips, but they love getting a good bargain at an op shop so it's not too much skin off their nose! My dad is definitely my biggest fan; he takes me to all my events, he takes me op-shopping (even if it's hours away), and he helps me with *everything*!

FDL: What makes you feel Opshopulent?

IF: Definitely having such freedom in my style! I have the coolest parents who let me wear whatever I want no matter how old I am, or how crazy they look walking next to me! I'm told I have a lot of courage for my age, and I'm completely open to learning more about sustainability!

What makes me feel most Opshopulent is the fact that I love what I do. Whenever I'm in an op shop I get a rush of excitement because I know that I'm helping someone, and I'm making a difference in someone else's life, which is seriously the most beautiful feeling! In the sustainable fashion community, not only do I get to learn new tips and tricks to assist with my second hand lifestyle, but I get to share *my* tips, tricks, and experiences with such a kind and accepting group of people!

Being able to see the beauty in second hand clothing is such a gift. Not many people my age can, and I'm so blessed that I get to show my generation that you can make an item from an op shop just as beautiful and fashionable as a first-hand item!

CHAPTER THIRTEEN

Opshopulence Interview Series

While op shopping plays a huge part in the second hand conversation, sustainability has many expressions. I am so fortunate to be surrounded by amazing thought leaders who have opened my eyes to a whole host of wonderful new ways to see the 'old.' They are the very example of visionary and exactly what the world needs right now. This chapter contains transcripts of conversations I had with the following people:

Carry Somers—Co-Founder *Fashion Revolution*
Juanita Erdedi—*Adaptive Clothing*
Emily Kate Symes, Ekoluv—*Why Buy When You Can Rent?*
Victoria Anthony—*Transgender Fashion*
Matt Davis, CEO Salvos Stores—*The Charity Retail Sector*
Kate McGuire—*The Converted Closet*
Veronica Pome'e—*Polynesian body positivity activist and curve model*
Patrick Duffy, Swap Chain—*Keeping Our Style In The Loop*
Kira Simpson—*The Green Hub*
Edwina Morgan, Head of Strategy Salvos Stores—*The Op Shop Evolution*
Aife O'loughlin, Customer experience manager—*What The Conscious Consumer Wants*

Carry Somers,
Fashion Revolution

FDL: Carry, I am so thrilled to connect with you. Could we start with you giving the readers a snapshot of how The Fashion Revolution movement, founded by you and Orsola de Castro, came to be?

CS: Fashion Revolution was founded in the aftermath of the Rana Plaza factory collapse in Bangladesh in 2013 when 1138 died and thousands more were injured. When I saw activists physically searching through the rubble to prove which brands were producing there, it was evident that the fashion industry needed revolutionary change. Over time, the crazy idea I had in the bath one day grew into the world's largest fashion activism movement. We now have teams in almost one hundred countries around the world and work all year round to mobilize citizens, industry and policy makers through our research, education and advocacy.

FDL: It's absolutely incredible to see the traction Fashion Revolution has had, the momentum and change it has created. I would love to know some of your most proud shape-shifting moments with the movement thus far.

CS: Every time I look at social media and see photographs of people holding **#imadeyourclothes** posters, I feel very proud to have helped provide visibility and amplification to the stories of the weavers, dyers, embroiderers, cotton farmers, seamstresses, spinners, union leaders and all the other people who make our clothing and accessories around the world.

On a personal level, I am very proud of sailing over 2000 miles from the Galapagos to Easter Island in Spring 2020 as part of eXXpedition to investigate and raise awareness of the devastating environmental impacts of plastics and toxics in the oceans. Textiles are estimated to be the largest source of microplastics, accounting for some 35% of global microplastic pollution. We launched a new hashtag **#whatsinmyclothes** to demand materials that don't generate significant environmental impacts, leak microfibers into our oceans and compromise human health and ecosystems.

FDL: How do you think we are going as a collective, as an industry? As the eco-stylist for the Salvos for the past eight years, I have definitely seen a shift, an awakening... but I know we still have much work to do. What do you think are still the stumbling blocks?

CS: While we are starting to see brands publish more about their social and environmental efforts, they continue to sidestep responsibility for safeguarding human rights and the rights of nature. While supply-chain workers struggle to earn a living wage and lead dignified lives, people of color, minorities and women are devalued, we fall far short of climate change targets, extract resources at an unsustainable speed and pollute our land and our oceans, the world's biggest fashion brands are getting steadily richer. This needs to change. Brands need to do a lot more to ensure shareholder profit is not prioritized above the health and wellbeing of workers and their communities and the protection of precious ecosystems.

FDL: Has sustainability always been a focus for you from a young age, or did you have an eco-awakening like I did?

CS: I think I was probably the first person to put the words *fair trade* and *fashion* together back in 1992 so, yes, you could say it has always been a focus. As part of my research for an MA in Native American Studies, I travelled to Ecuador to study traditional textile and dyeing skills. I was not prepared for the inequitable trading patterns I witnessed. Seeing the weighing scales, an international symbol of justice, being loaded with wool on one side and the producers being charged a price which bore no resemblance to the cost per kilo, I felt a sense of outrage at the clear discrimination before me. Quechua speakers with only rudimentary Spanish and low levels of numeracy were at the mercy of the middlemen when it came to buying the wool and selling their finished knitwear. I met two groups of workers who had organized themselves into cooperatives, but both had experienced arson attacks due to the threat they posed to the intermediaries' monopoly of the supply chain. The next summer, I returned to Ecuador and gave them the financial resources to buy raw materials in bulk and, despite having no background in design, produced a series of knitwear patterns that sold out in six weeks. Seeing the tangible difference to the producers' livelihoods encouraged me to give up my PhD and concentrate on improving the lives of more producers in the Andean region with my brand, Pachacuti.

FDL: In my book, *Opshopulence*, I talk about the concept that sustainability has to be sustainable for us, as individuals. I really resonated with your recent Instagram post about your McQueen dress and why you never wear blue. We'd love to hear your musings on this.

CS: I don't wear blue, although sometimes I wish I did. I still half-regret not buying a beautiful indigo-dyed dress in Oaxaca. I have two blue items in my wardrobe. Yes, two. I recently posted a photograph of myself wearing my faithful painting dungarees which I've had for 20 years or more. I also have a pair of wide-legged indigo linen trousers that I wear for sailing and these must be 25 years old or more. Creating a sustainable wardrobe is, in part, knowing what you will wear time and time again, year after year. On the day in question, after I'd finished painting, I put on an Alexander McQueen bodycon dress made from superfine wool. Bought from a sample sale, over the last decade I have worn it to numerous speaking events, but sometimes team it with wellington boots for walking the dog. That evening I mended a hole in its seam. It packs into nothing and even came on my sailing voyage this year, when space was at a real premium, worn for talks in Mexico City, Quito, and Santiago. It never needs washing. I love it. Don't get me wrong, choosing the right materials, supporting artisanal, fair trade and sustainable brands are all incredibly important, but if the garment sits languishing at the back of your wardrobe, it's not that sustainable. It may be that I could buy that indigo dress and learn to love the color, but do I want to take that chance? I'm not a fan of **#30wears** or however many wears it is. I want to know that I'll be wearing and sharing my clothes for a decade or more, and ideally for most of my lifetime. And that's why I don't buy blue.

FDL: Do you feel women are driving this movement, or do you see a strong male presence stepping up too? I adore the *Ode to the Women of the Earth* by Amanda Gorman, featured in your Fashion Revolution mag, *Fanzine*—it really drives home my belief that individual impact is powerful, we have the innate ability to create change, and if we all use our voice, serious progress can prevail. What are some simple ways each of us can step up and do better?

CS: The need for citizens to use their voices and power to hold brands and retailers to account is more pressing than ever before. We need to ask the question **#whomademyclothes** and demand an industry free from child labor, forced labor, and all forms of exploitation. We also need to ask **#whatsinmyclothes** and ask brands to use materials that don't generate massive environmental impacts, leak microfibers into our oceans and compromise human health and nature's ecosystems. Fashion Revolution's website has many resources and reports, from our annual Fashion Transparency Index to Get Involved packs with details of all the actions you can take. We also run online courses, such as our MOOC on Fashion's Future and the Sustainable Development Goals.

While I agree that individual impact is powerful, and we often underestimate our ability to bring about change, individual actions are not enough to bring about the systemic change needed to end the exploitation of people and the planet in the global fashion industry. We must join forces because we are louder, more powerful and stand a better chance of achieving change when we work together.

Beyond cultural change, we will also need the industry to take urgent collaborative action to be more transparent, pay their workers fairly, protect the people throughout their supply chains and restore our living planet. Governments must also play a more active role in regulating the industry and better enforcing laws that already exist to protect workers and the environment.

FDL: Opshopulence is a mindset, seeing that true beauty and abundance is in a wardrobe which makes a difference to the world. What makes you feel Opshopulent?

CS: I buy a lot of my clothes from designers in Mexico who work directly with artisan communities. When I visit, I often give them my size, design and color choice, and wait. Sometimes six months, sometimes a year later, my hand-embroidered skirt or dress will arrive. These are garments I will always treasure. I'm not really a believer in **#30wears**, more like **#30years**.

FDL: I like to call the space we orbit in Future Fashion, it's the business model we must move towards—circularity, kindness, inclusivity, community. What do you see/hope/plan for the future of fashion?

CS: I have spent all of my spare time in the last ten months writing a book.

The story begins at Crebilly Castle in 1787 when the notorious womanizer and Protestant squire entices a French Catholic orphan to his home to take up a fictitious offer of employment, looking simply for another trinket to be dangled and discarded. In doing so, he sets in motion an extraordinary saga of seduction, betrayal, bigamy, multiple deceptions, debtors' prison, discrimination, a lost inheritance, and a scandal that rocked Irish society. I grew up hearing about the story of the Squire and the Frenchwoman—they are my fourth great grandparents—but I had no idea until I began my research that Madeleine was a lacemaker.

Now she walks around with me in my head every day as I draw parallels between her story and the working conditions of millions of garment workers around the world. Madeleine reminds me that some things have changed very little for the people who make our clothes in the last two hundred years. As Madeleine fell into debt when her husband abandoned her and she had to support herself through lacemaking and dressmaking, so millions of the people who make our clothes are having to borrow money to get from one payday to the next. Living wages still feel so far off in the fashion industry and I want to see brands do more, and urgently, to guarantee their workers the right to a decent living. I may not be able to alter the multiple injustices suffered by my ancestors, but I can certainly play my part in helping to ensure that all of today's garment workers see a better future.

Juanita Erdedi
Adaptive Clothing

FDL: There seems to be so many examples of brands not waking up, and they're not realizing there's this whole community of people who, for them, getting dressed is difficult. Tell me about some of the challenges you face with dressing Simone?

JE: Well she's better now because she's older but there's still a lot of things that she can't wear. Like she can't wear heels, she can't wear sandals, not for long. They might look good when she puts them on but she can't walk because she has flat feet, and she can't hold her weight so she needs something that supports her. That's what the biggest issue for us has always been—the walking. She took three and a half years to walk.

I found zippers weren't too bad but she was always scared of them, scared of pinching herself. Buttons, shoes and straps are still a problem. For school she couldn't wear laces ever. They had to be Velcro. She can do laces now, she learnt over the years but she still has trouble; it will take her a while to do them up. So she's really not as bad as some people but it's always been finding things that were easy for her.

FDL: But you can't find them, right? So what did you do?

JE: Well I fixed a lot of things myself. I put Velcro on things that I felt were easier for her to put on. I took buttons off things that she just couldn't do up. I was lucky that I could sew. Not every mum with a daughter like Simone can do that though. I used a lot of knitted stuff because you could just pull it on and off. A lot of pants I turned elastic.

FDL: Just like Mindy from Runway of Dreams, it's almost like you have to become Martha Stewart to empower your child.

JE: Yes! I wanted her to wear what everyone else was. I wanted her to wear jeans and to wear the uniform like everyone else. I didn't want her to wear different clothes to school because she couldn't wear the proper uniform.

I did fix a lot of the clothes because when she had to go to the toilet, she couldn't do up the pants. So I would take off the zippers, sew them up and then make them bigger, add elastic. And I always made sure she had a top over it so you wouldn't see the fixes. But honestly, she always looked beautiful and I always tried to make feel beautiful too, but it was difficult. I'll never forget what this woman, a good friend of mine, said to me. Simone was wearing a stunning long dress, and my 'friend' said, 'Oh my God she looks so beautiful, everything is perfect except her shoes. Why couldn't she wear little high heels?'

And I said, 'Oh my goodness, are you kidding me? Do you honestly think that I would not let her wear them if she could!?'

FDL: Do you ever see brands talking about this now? Do you go into a store and see any adaptive clothing?

JE: No. It's not there, and if it is I wanna know where it is because I've never seen it. And by the way, I have to say she tends to dress a little bit better because of her sister Natalie.

FDL: Do you see it affect Simone's confidence? Have you seen moments where she's frustrated because she can't wear certain things? Have you seen her look insecure because of a piece of clothing?

JE: Yes! She loves short skirts. I can't put skirts on her because she doesn't know how to sit. So she has to wear a long skirt, and then if she's wearing a long skirt what shoes will she wear? She'll always ask me for them, and crop tops, but she can't—she's got to have items that cover her tummy. I want her to look elegant.

FDL: Do you know what I do with crop tops!? I wear a men's button-down underneath. I have a satin bralette that I love to layer and wear it as outer wear. Talking about adaptive clothing, I adapt clothing for my body too, in a way. I feel like there are different ways Simone could tap into it too. It seems to be with writing this book, this universal discovery for me that clothing is so powerful in how it can make us feel, but how it can really hinder us too. It just amazes me that brands have not thought of this, especially not in Australia anyway.

JE: Oh yes! I really believe that, so true. It's always Europe that thinks of things before we do. But by now—Simone is 33 years old—there's still nothing really out there. You get the sizes 8-16 and after that you get the big sizes but that's also the problem I've always had. Lucky I can sew! Everything is too long 'cause she's got very short arms and short legs, so everything I get her is too long. I've always had to fix sleeves and hems. I was so happy when the short leg denim came out.

FDL: So where do you shop for Simone? Where do you go?

JE: I don't buy expensive things for her because of her anxiety. She breaks her clothes, unpicks hems and stitches. I find Target, I know it's not a great sustainable brand but it has short lengths, wider pants, I can find more there than anywhere else.

FDL: I think the thing with sustainability—and this is something I really discovered, too—it must be sustainable for *you*. Especially when brands are not really giving you a choice. Like if there was an eco-friendly adaptive clothing brand for disabled people you would go there, right?

JE: OMG, that would be my shop!

FDL: But your choices are limited because the industry is not catering to your child.

JE: I also wonder if those shops were around would they be really expensive? Because if they were then people with disabilities wouldn't wear them. It defeats the purpose. Most of them are living on a pension if they are adults. Some of them have no families and they live in homes. Can they afford this? So I think that when it does come to this country, it would have to be affordable for all of these people.

FDL: Do you ever go to second hand stores or thrift stores for Simone?

JE: I've been to a few nice ones. My other daughter Natalie was really into thrifting for a while, as she was trying to find her identity as a gay woman, and in all honesty I've seen Natalie struggle more than Simone with clothes and feeling herself in clothes!

FDL: Wow, that's fascinating. This is why I love thrifting so much—no division, no judgment, just an opportunity to play and find your expression!

JE: Yes, exactly! It really helped Natalie. I don't shop much, in fact I get all my clothes handed down from my daughter! I take all the leftovers! She hands me down all the things she doesn't wear anymore. I love it! It makes me feel young. Some things I can fix for Simone. Some of the shirts might have darts in the back, so I just undo them and it's bigger for me!

FDL: You're naturally sustainable! I love that you're all sharing! I think it's so inspiring because hand-me-downs normally go the other way—from the older to the younger, but you guys have got this cool reverse situation going on and you're making it sustainable for you. I think that's really cool.

JE: I get so excited. Some people are like 'oh old clothes', but not me. I go through them all. I can fix this and I can do that, so I cut dresses and reinvent things.

FDL: So what would you say to brands in terms of Simone and thinking about adaptability? Is there a message you would want to give to them?

JE: Do something. Wake up to yourselves. There are all types of people. You cater for larger—beautiful, thank you! Now can you cater for people with disabilities? There's more by the way, more people with disabilities than there are large people, why can't they?

FDL: Why do you think they haven't? Why isn't adaptive clothing considered more?

JE: I think it's because it hasn't been that long that disabled people have been out there, it wasn't that long ago that you didn't really see people with disabilities out there. But now they go out more, they have more opportunities and consideration with work, more acceptance.

By the way, most of these people are dressed by someone else and they don't care... 'Oh here, these will do'. I have a lot of friends with kids with disabilities—and I would say to them: 'You know you can get jeans at X store and they're really cool' but they will always say: 'What for?'

You see, it's the parents too. But what about when you go out? Don't you want your kids to look and feel nice no matter their ability? It's like they think it's not worth it, they don't deserve it. That made me sad as a parent.

FDL: We need to get you as an adviser for a brand to make these people wake up. Honestly, you're so inspiring.

JE: I honestly think that it's about bloody time that someone thinks about people with disabilities. Not just kids, but adults; they want to go out dancing, they want to go to a pub and have fun and they want to look nice! They should be able to go into shops and feel like everybody else. How can they feel good when they have to wear ugly, outdated clothes? It doesn't matter who you are or what state you're in, clothes can change how we feel. They want to belong; they want to be like everybody else.

FDL: And girls of all ages and all sizes and all abilities, we all love to feel pretty. Even if we say that we don't, like whatever that means for you we all like to feel good. Do you see that with Simone too?

JE: Omg, she loves it when someone gives her a compliment. I was talking to her the other day on FaceTime when she was at her sister's, and I said, 'Ohhh Simmy, you look so beautiful today, what are you wearing?' And she goes, 'Ohhhhh, thank you, Mum!' And when Natalie is looking after Simone she does her hair, and she looks even more fashionable.

FDL: It's so nice how you all work together to elevate her. It's beautiful.

JE: Oh, well she's so beautiful, she deserves it!

FDL: You're such a beautiful mum and human, Juanita. Thank you for sharing your story.

Emily Kate Symes
EKOLUV

FDL: Tell us about your pre-loved passion, EKOLUV.

EKS: EKOLUV is Australia's first zero-waste sustainable, dress hire and consignment boutique situated on the infamous William Street, in Paddington, Sydney. EKOLUV aims to close the loop and prolong the lifespan of fashion already in existence rather than buying new. In turn creating less waste and saving on our precious resources. Everything in our boutique is either second hand, diverted from landfill or upcycled, right down to the wooden hangers and our clothing racks!

Driven by an authentic commitment to social justice and environmental responsibility, we aim to change people's perception that luxury has to mean 'new.' We offer customers the opportunity to buy vintage and second hand, as well as to rent clothing. You will find second hand designer dresses available to buy at a fraction of the retail price, and the latest designer dresses available to rent for those special occasions. We are all about empowering women and mindful of those who don't have the same opportunities. That's why we have chosen to partner with Opportunity International Australia and donate 5% of our profits towards the cause.

FDL: How or what made you choose a more conscious fashion path?

EKS: Since I was a little girl, I have always been into vintage and second hand fashion. I used to rummage through the op shops with my mother looking for treasures, and treasures I found indeed. This was a way for me to connect with my mother and sparked a love affair with fashion that has been with me my whole life. My mum's wedding dress to my stepdad was from an op shop and cost her only $6! I remember her looking a million bucks and thinking, wow you don't have to compromise on looking good buying second hand.

In a recent report from St. Vincent De Paul Society, the average Australian woman consumes 27 kgs of clothing per year, only uses about 33% of what's actually in her wardrobe and throws away 23kgs of that amount away per year. I founded EKOLUV in 2012 out of frustration that I was unable to find a way to shop luxury fashion in a sustainable way. Working as a model at the time, I saw first-hand the excess waste the industry produced and also the cost to the garment makers and damage the industry was having on the environment and people's lives. It got me thinking, what is my own impact? I then looked at my own consumer footprint and realized I had unsustainable shopping habits and a wardrobe bursting with pieces still with tags on I hadn't even worn.

FDL: What was life like before your style awakening?

EKS: When I was a teenager, even though I loved op shopping and had a love affair with vintage and pre-loved clothes, I felt the pressure to buy fast-fashion and so found myself buying a lot of things I didn't need. In my 20s, however, that all changed when I reconnected with my true self and love for nature and started to embrace high-end luxury fashion that was made well and made to last and re-verged back to my pre-loved clothing obsession. So now my style is a mix of both pre-loved and high-end designer wear.

FDL: Could you speak on the concept of style being transformational and how you've seen that play out in your life personally?

EKS: It allows me to be creative and express myself. It's amazing how a good outfit can improve your mood and set you up for the day ahead. It definitely makes me happier, saved me so much money and feel more connected to my clothing as I choose to invest in quality pieces and therefore, I value my clothes a lot more.

FDL: What makes you feel Opshopulent?

EKS: I feel Opshopulent and eco-chic the most when I'm wearing my best pre-loved outfit and people love my outfit and comment 'Where did you get it from?' and I'm so proud I tell them I got it from Salvos for like $4. I always feel so accomplished and love the reactions people give like, 'Wow, you wouldn't tell that's from an op shop.' I also feel most Opshopulent when I'm around my good friends and tribe of women such as you Faye!

FDL: Share with us resources that really helped you on your journey—books, podcasts, individuals, practices etc., and what wisdom would you impart to someone new to this space or wanting to join in?

EKS: Educate yourself as much as you can and do your research. Don't buy into 'green washing', a lot of these big fashion companies are putting out there. Be discerning! I would recomend:

- *This is A Good Guide* by Marieke Eyeskroot
- *Eco Renaissance*, Marci Zaroff
- *The True Cost* documentary, Minimalism documentary.
- You my love! Faye De Lanty
- Red Carpet Green Dress
- Eco Age and **#30wears,** Livia Firth

I encourage others to "Be the change you wish to see in the world" (Mahatma Gandhi). This is my favorite quote because it always reminds me that change lies within, that if I want to change the world around me, I have to start with myself first. The genesis for change is awareness. We cannot change what we don't acknowledge. By becoming more aware we begin the process of change.

FDL: I would love to hear a sneaky style elevation trick you may have. How do you make second hand look first class for your own outfits?

EKS: Steaming them, also using a good quality leather conditioner on any pre-loved bags I have; it gives them a shine and makes them look brand new. Also adding accessories to any pre-loved outfit to elevate the look.

FDL: I like to call what we do 'future fashion.' What do you predict for the future of pre-loved chic, especially post-COVID?

EKS: For all the challenges COVID posed to our assumptions about consumer behavior, one thing is clear: consumers everywhere are prioritizing sustainability now more than ever when making a fashion purchase or spring cleaning their wardrobe. Pre-owned, refurbished, repaired, and rental business models continue to evolve. Consumers are demonstrating an appetite to shift away from traditional ownership to newer ways in which to access products as seen by the success of EKOLUV.

In fashion, the shift to new ownership models is driven by growing consumer desire for variety, sustainability, and affordability, and sources suggest that the resale market, for instance, could be bigger than fast-fashion within ten years.

Finally, the younger generation is seen to be more powerful than ever before as they are now realizing that they literally vote for the kind of world they want with their dollar. They are becoming more mindful of their consumer footprint and are actively showing a genuine desire to be part of the long-term solution to fashion waste. This inspires much optimism ahead for not just our local community but for the planet as a whole.

> 'Each purchase we make or not make, in turn makes a statement and shapes the way our world operates and what we want our future to look like.'
>
> Emily Kate Symes @ekoluv

Miss Victoria Anthony
Transgender Fashion

FDL: How has fashion empowered you on your journey to authentic self-expression?

VA: Going from living as a boy to becoming a gorgeous girl, I had to relearn how to dress. I feel like the clothes I wear nowadays really help shape my identity as a woman. I know not everyone might feel the same, but I love to embrace my femininity and I express that by wearing a lot of high-glam, dresses, makeup, heels, accessories. I love it! It really helps me feel confident.

FDL: On the flip side of that, have there been moments fashion has hindered you, held you back?

VA: I feel like being a transgender woman comes with people judging your level of femininity and I feel that pressure but I'm slowly learning to embrace different styles and not being so high-glam and sexy all the time, I recently started sharing my gym attire in my exercise videos, no makeup and completely different to what I normally post online. I want to show different sides to me and own the different clothing I can wear.

FDL: Do you feel represented in the fashion industry?

VA: Not really, honestly. And I know a lot of other transgender women who might struggle finding clothes that fit them. There are no major fashion lines or high fashion for transgender people. Hopefully one day. There's also not as many transgender models out there in comparison to the broader spectrum but we are out and proud and I'm sure there's more to come in future, watch this space.

FDL: Has thrifting, second hand and or DIY/customizing been something you've explored with the clothing you wear or create for your work?

VA: Yes definitely, I love to re-wear my clothes a lot and I actually buy a lot of clothes regularly but I never just throw them away after I wear them. I regift them to other transgender women and they wear them to death and then pass them along too. I have a lot of stuff that girls wouldn't buy for themselves and the girls I give stuff to always feel so proud to say that it's from Victoria Anthony. They look so confident and empowered when they wear the clothes.

FDL: You are such a beacon of light for the trans community. What message would you like to share with my readers and the fashion community at large?

VA: Own it. Rock it. There's no wrong way to be transgender. Wear whatever you want. Live it up! Be proud of who you are. Inspire others to live their truth.

Matt Davis
CEO Salvos Stores
—The Charity Retail Sector

FDL: Matt, you are the National Director of Salvos Stores, and it's a pleasure being part of the team with you at the helm. You have such a shape-shifting vision for the charity retail sector!

Can you speak to us a little more about your role, what it involves and what you want the op shopping experience to become?

MD: As National Director, my responsibility is to ensure that Salvos Stores plays its part in sustaining the Salvation Army's mission of giving 'hope where it's needed most' well into the future. In a practical sense this means I get to lead a team of incredibly passionate people in enabling literally millions of Australians to make a positive social and environmental impact. Australia has moved well beyond the days where op shopping was a cottage industry and a bit socially taboo. Today over 200,000 Australians come into one of our stores every week, raising millions of dollars of funding and diverting tens of thousands of tons from landfill each year. This means that the role of National Director is ultimately about leadership, strategy, culture and building a vision that our communities can be proud of in years to come.

While I'd love to see the op shopping experience become one that appeals to Australians from every walk of life, I hope it never loses that sense of local community connection. Op shops are essentially a social contract with local communities that promise if you invest your donations, your time as a volunteer or your shopping dollar, that charities will deliver positive impact in ways that are important to you. This contract has to be at the center of everything we do. So whether it be enabling a circular economy, innovating online, or keeping those connections with regular customers, the experience of the future will always need to remain authentic.

FDL: Would you break down the process for us, from donation to shop floor, and give some insight into where the money goes and who/how it helps?

MD: The process starts with our amazing donors. Once they have arranged a home collection, post-in satchel or dropped off their items during opening hours, our team start the sorting process straight away. Processing donations locally gives our teams the opportunity to identify the items they know local customers are looking for. Once the decision has been made on what items are appropriate for sale, products make their way to the shop floor on a daily basis and go through a four-week rotation cycle. Most items are sold after a final level of discounting, with a small amount removed from sale to join the items that were unsuitable upon donation. Whether these items are damaged, soiled or simply not in demand, our team separates the products into their different recycling streams—electronics, metals, paper/cardboard, textiles and so on. We work with a range of partners both within Australia and overseas to ensure that these items enter the best resource recovery path we can access. Unfortunately, some items such as soft toys, soft furnishings and heavily soiled donations do not yet have resource recovery options across Australia and enter the general waste stream. We are always on the lookout for new ways to recycle, so if anyone out there knows of any emerging opportunities, please let us know!

In terms of where the money goes, 100% of the profits of Salvos Stores support programs run by the Salvation Army. The Salvos provide over one million episodes of care to vulnerable Australians every year in areas such as emergency supplies for those doing it tough, recovery support from natural disasters, alcohol and other drug rehabilitation programs, and family violence services. This is the amazing thing about op shops, by simply donating your pre-loved items or buying second hand, you are doing something positive for both people and planet!

FDL: Recycling, sustainability and social impact are big passions of yours. Have they always been a part of your DNA? What drew you to them?

MD: Like most of the passions in our lives, they are handed down by those people who have influenced us the most. I have had the privilege of being associated with the Salvation Army my whole life and seen many facets of the amazing work they do first-hand. Both of my grandmothers volunteered in different community groups and also worked in their local op shop. I remember tagging along during school holidays and receiving the strangest of gifts from time to time. Our family still laughs about the year Nanna gave me a used Teledex for Christmas! The idea of 'loving your neighbor as yourself' has always been a huge part of our family's values and my faith, so I guess it's no surprise where I ended up!

FDL: Salvos Stores helps to support over one million people a year. As National Director you must have seen some incredible stories of hope. Is there one that really stands out and drives home the transformational power op shopping can have on community?

MD: There is such a wide variety of impact that flows from having op shops in our community. There are obviously the lives changed through funded programs and the unwanted items that find their way into a second life. What I am particularly inspired by is the transformation that happens within the four walls of each shop. There are so many Australians who come into a store just because it is a safe place. When I was in Adelaide a couple of years ago, I met a mother who spends a day each week sitting on the lounges in our furniture section. Our Store Manager explained to me that her 30-year-old son had an acquired brain injury from a motor vehicle accident and that he only remembered his father, not his mother. So that her son didn't become distressed during their visits to the care facility each week, her husband would drop her at the store for the day. While devastating, she felt safe and welcome by our team. It was a very special moment for me to understand the many ways lives can be transformed. It is my hope that these examples of human connection, one life at a time, always remain true for us.

FDL: A huge portion of what Salvos Stores sells to support the mission of the Salvation Army is second hand textiles, which makes the organization an urban recycler to be reckoned with. Lord knows we need it with the stats telling us that the average Australian throws out 23 kgs of clothing every year. How much clothing does Salvos Stores divert from landfill annually? What happens to the items we can't recycle?

MD: Fashion and other textiles have always been a huge part of the op shop experience. Representing about half of all the items we sell, Salvos Stores diverts about 20,000 tons every year. Due to the effects of fast-fashion and the prosperity enjoyed by Australians generally, the volume of clothing that charities receive has for a number of years required recycling solutions beyond what can be sold through the stores or online. Charities work with a range of commercial textile recyclers who export, sort, re-use and recycle these items. There is a significant global market for second hand textiles and while it is certainly evolving, many emerging economies will continue to seek affordable goods designed for more advanced markets. It is encouraging to see new technologies emerging to process textiles that genuinely have reached the end of their usable life and many charities and commercial recyclers are collaborating to prepare the way for a truly global circular economy.

FDL: What do you think are still obstacles for some consumers, why don't they op shop? Why don't they donate/donate-consciously, and how can charity retailers like Salvos Stores be of service here?

MD: From my perspective, time will always be a barrier. The op shop experience is fundamentally different in the sense that you never know what you will find. While for many customers the thrill of the chase is part of the fun, other customers too time constrained will be happy to pay a premium for on-demand experiences. It is great to see charities like the Salvos really stepping up in the online space to make shopping faster and more convenient. So while this may close the gap and broaden the appeal of op shops for some, there will always be other offers out there that will simply deliver a faster end-to-end experience.

A big opportunity that I know you're passionate about, Faye, is about bringing things that may seem exclusive within reach. For many customers seeking a high-end experience, op shops may seem unable to fit the bill. I believe that through the advocacy of key influencers, learning how to pull a great outfit together and op shops continuing to improve how they curate on-trend items, we can continue to help Australians see new possibilities.

FDL: I know that over the seven years I've been working with Salvos Stores I've seen a huge shift and growth in the popularity of op shopping. Second hand is seriously on the rise! I love that you continue to guide your team to move with these times. Case in point, the COVID pivot with creating an online platform for people to op shop from their couch—complete genius. Tell us about the digital hub!?

MD: Thanks, Faye! We really do have an incredible team who stepped up right across the country during the COVID-19 pandemic to take our online offering to the next level. Our online journey started over five years ago, so we have had the chance to experience quite a bit of trial and error. We were fortunate to have invested in some key people and platforms over the last couple of years that gave us the foundation to build on during the period our stores were closed. Our digital hub is essentially the team that powers everything we do for e-commerce. Based at our warehouse in Melbourne, they facilitate a number of different options for customers, including the ability for over 100 of our stores around the country to list and ship items directly, click and collect in certain locations, and a dedicated eBay store for collectibles and other unique items. But the journey won't end there! There is no doubt that second hand online retail still has significant opportunities in the years ahead. We are well underway in introducing more stores, digital hubs and other ways for our customers to both shop and donate digitally. Imagine all the social and environmental impact we can have together if customers can choose how they wish to engage any time of day or night!

FDL: I like to call what we do 'future fashion.' What do you predict and hope for the future of pre-loved and conscious chic, especially post-COVID?

MD: One of the ways I like to think about the future is to imagine how people will use the things they buy and sell today. This includes thinking about the wardrobe of the future. I believe that things won't sit in our wardrobes quite so long. We'll turn them over more quickly, knowing it's perfectly possible to share, rent, donate, upcycle and recycle these items. I believe consumers will continue to demand fashion that is not only stylish but thoughtful in its design, using materials that are ethically sourced, last long enough to be reused many times and can be easily repaired and ultimately remanufactured into other items. I hope that as we go on this journey together that we do so knowing that it is within the power of every individual to positively influence the lives of those around them by the choices they make each and every day.

Kate McGuire
The Converted Closet

@convertedcloset

FDL: Thank you to the Instagram gods for connecting us, because you are incredibly cool, my lady! Could you tell everyone about your genius mission to get the world converting their clothes?

KM: Thank you Faye! My mission is born from a lifelong passion that now turns out to be immensely planet friendly—the stars have aligned!

I like to say I 'convert' clothes rather than 'upcycle' them—it feels and sounds more luxurious, to wear something 'converted'—do you know what I mean? Essentially, converting is *design-led upcycling*—I don't just aim to give garments new life, I intend to elevate them to realize their maximum potential! They need to be as desirable to me as luxury designer pieces.

You and I know it's entirely possible to have your luxe clothing cake and eat it, served on a big beautiful GREEN plate... but we need to prove it to the masses! The consumer jury is still out because so few people are upcycling at a luxury level.

My mission is to prove the endless possibilities of converting clothes to inspire people to create their own beautiful, high-end pieces using nothing but what's already in existence. Ultimately clothes are simply pieces of fabric that can be reshaped, so if there's something we're not keen on about a garment, why on earth wouldn't we alter it to create exactly what we like instead? Almost anything is possible—from changing easy component parts like necklines and sleeves, to radically transforming the makeup of a garment—dress into jumpsuit anyone? It's literally a win-win-win, with our precious planet being the ultimate beneficiary. What's not to love?!

According to the Ellen McArthur Foundation (oh how I love her!), extending the lifecycle of clothes is singularly the most sustainable action we can all take to reduce the fashion industry's horrendous contribution to the climate crisis. Clearly, we're all going to wear our clothes more if we love and value them, so why not create things we never want to take off by converting to personal perfection?

FDL: How or what made you choose a more conscious fashion path?

KM: I started converting clothes out of desperation and necessity, not knowing how this would lead to the most important epiphany of my life.

Having had a perpetual, very painful battle with my weight and body for years, I became deeply depressed, grieving that I couldn't present myself to the world in the way I wanted to—completely trapped by food addiction. So out of frustration, I started to play around with clothes to try to make them work for my body, just the way it was, rather than against it. Through experimenting, I found I could exaggerate the parts of my body I liked, disguise those I didn't and add my own unique twist. I discovered I felt more awesome in my Dad's oversized converted, hacked dinner shirt than any off-the-peg fast-fashion. I felt empowered and my confidence grew—as did the compliments. I realized that my style sweetspot exists right on The Very Edge. And I finally had access.

My eco-aha moment came out of nowhere. I'd been as 'green' as the average decent citizen in following recycling rules but honestly just hadn't come to understand enough about environmental issues to embrace the movement wholeheartedly. I'd started an instagram feed, encouraged by my hairdresser who showed me the ropes during a blow-dry, just to share my love of converting clothes and show what's possible to maximize closet fun—and cash. I've always had consumer anxiety and this way I'd learnt to maximize both bang and buck. It was only after someone suggested I watch "The True Cost" that the fashion world I'd been deeply in love with for my lifetime, suddenly shattered. That film singlehandedly turned my obsession from vivid technicolor to monochrome in less than two hours. But it was only when I found myself compulsively transcribing the entire film on a flight from London to New York that the pieces fell into place. We're producing 150 billion new clothes every year to satiate the appetites of just 8 billion people, using up precious finite natural resources and unethical human labour to do so? It was so hard to take in as made absolutely no sense—what about our future?!

Knowing how to create highly desirable new clothes in a totally 'safe' way seemed odd—why wasn't anyone else talking about this?

In the drive to inform myself, I attended the Copenhagen Fashion Summit in 2019, then enrolled at Cambridge University to qualify in Business Sustainability Leadership and finally completed a deep-dive in Sustainable Fashion at Harvard after a family relocation to New York. Covering all angles has given me confidence in the subject and the ability to spot greenwashing a mile off. Behind the rails, it's the absolute antithesis of glamour and we all need to do everything we can if we're to actually have a fashion industry in 50 years.

If things are really going to change, we have to find a way of giving fashion-loving consumers what they want in an impact-free way and I've realised, actually what better way is there than to convert? Billions of fabulous pre-owned clothes aching for conversion are now so easy to access online—and in our very own closets! We know 'cool' sells and people seem to love conversions, so why not create clothes cool enough to rival new designer pieces with zero impact and prove that there's a whole new world out there?! Wearing conversion is a badge of sustainabilty-honor and speak volumes.

I always feel so proud of what I wear—converted clothes are imbued with extra feel-good.

FDL: I just adore what you do—it has such a high-end feel. I really identify with the shape-shifting nature... it's Opshopulence personified. Could you speak on second-hand and sustainability perceptions and how it's time to bust them and make it beautiful?

KM: I love your term Opshopulence! I actually think we are well on our way to busting the perception that second hand is somehow 'less-than' new. The stigma is rightfully dying out and I've noticed the change toward pre-owned is especially dramatic in the US where it's been looked down upon for so long. My husband would never have considered wearing anything second-hand when I met him 12 years ago (he literally thought it was slightly grim—but loved what I wore... slightly confusing!) But now I buy him sweaters from Opshops and he loves that I do! Like others, he's just realized—the clothes are exactly the same and often not even worn.

I was in a fancy NY restaurant recently and a smart lady my mother's age was on the next table wearing a dress with a huge "The Real Real" brand tag hanging down her back. That's a very positive sign of the times I thought (before helping her yank it off)! Pre-owed is truly the NEW new for all generations.

People who are designing and creating 'new' from pre-owned clothes realize just what's possible—it really is time to help and inspire everyone to get on board the sustainability train and experience the joy of converting clothes. I get stopped constantly by people commenting on what I'm wearing—my family zone it out! Fundamentally, it's a question of educating people and there's nothing more powerful than doing that through entertainment—I need to make a show! People deserve to know about this—when they experience the satisfaction it brings they'll never look back, will they? We know it!

Converting doesn't mean compromising on luxury—I'll never wear anything that doesn't look and feel divine. I went to an event at Annabel's in London last year to see Edward Enninful (Editor, British Vogue) in conversation with Sarah Harris (Deputy Editor). I wore a converted outfit and and spent a substantial part of the evening fielding the same question:

who made the dress?... "No way!!"

FDL: Is your sustainability work influencing your day to day choices?

KM: Absolutely! I'm so thankful for the environmental awakening I had because life feels rich and so meaningful now knowing that I'm personally helping to reduce environmental impact. Everything I convert into something new creates one more alternative to buying new: deep sigh of relief! (Clearly I need to start selling now!!) Being more conscious of how all our actions have a knock-on affect on the planet has affected my family too: my husband now asks whether I have a bag with me when I go grocery shopping which I don't think that will ever stop surprising me—I LOVE it! Our 9-year old is incredulous that as a population we're not doing more in the face of a catastrophic climate crisis, and my darling twin step-daughters take immense pleasure in flexing their incredible Opshop finds! One of them is very involved in her prestigious university fashion magazine and has the most incredible unique style—I don't think she ever wears new! OpShop is guilt-free, great value and... drum roll... actually cooler. The kids are leading the charge.

I think a lot of people are addicted to 'fashion fix'—in a serious way. Addiction is obviously not a joke and the impact on our psyche of wearing new clothes is immense. To that end, I think telling people to 'buy less' is just falling on deaf ears a lot of the time. At least with converted clothes people can have the new fantastic, unique fashion they want with zero impact— whilst we all work on taming our insatiable appetites to get comfortable with the new less-is-more norm.

Fashion has at the benefit of such a powerful play that other industries don't have—it has beauty—the ultimate tool of persuasion. It can influence the masses through *attraction*—"catching more files with honey than vinegar." A trend can see a vast number of people suddenly adopting a new idea and behavior so when it becomes achingly cool to wear truly sustainable clothes, and uncool not to, change will speed up. Momentum is key which is honestly what drives me to get the message out to as many people as I can—I think entertaining them with a glamorous show (the honey) then educating them along the way is the way I could do it most effectively. What about you? (REALLY INTERESTING TO SEE YOUR ANSWER FAYE!)

There's also such massive commercial opportunity to be had round sustainability too right now—creating new value out of old clothing has such exciting money-making prospects. I think we'll look back on where we are now, in 10 years time with such different industrial 'circular' systems in place and the fashion capital will be held by different players—businesses that facilitate truly circular, planet-saving solutions, including tech.

I love that converting old clothes doesn't just prevent waste, it simultaneously reduces the consumption of new; two sides of the same coin. Companies have to listen to consumer demand or they'll go bust and given that the entire industry is based on a linear business model, there's understandable panic. I get it. My biggest learning from Cambridge however, was the understanding that *sustainability is innovation's new frontier.* There's so much proof now that sustainable practices are proving to yield both top and bottom-line returns. I absolutely love feeling like I'm an activist for a movement helping to usher in a whole new fashion industry paradigm — don't you? If I ever get a bit tired (it happens!) I only need to remember the WHY about all this and the mojo relights instantly.

FDL: What makes you feel Opshopulent?

KM: Fabric type is so important to me—nothing beats super-high quality natural vintage fibers. Pre fast-fashion materials are deliciously opulent and durable (thank God!). There are some really amazing synthetic fibers out there too though—the oldies are the besties I've found. I'm thinking of a gorgeous vintage satin polyester (former) dress I own made from an incredible, thick silky polyester I've never come across before—*stunning* fabric; it's my current favorite jaunty jumpsuit.

As long as it's good quality, great to look at and comfortable to wear, I'm in! When I convert, fabric often dictates the fundamental re-design which I guess makes me 'fabric and former-feature led!

Embracing such a wide range of different features already built into clothes to be converted makes for an eclectic collection. I often feel as if I'm working right alongside the original designer and together we're creating something new. It's such a lovely feeling—I'm never alone or stuck for ideas.

FDL: I love that you believe everyone can unleash their inner designer and that we don't have to wait to be a 'perfect' weight to wear an item—we can convert our wardrobes to fit us. This is music to my fashion ears, please share your thoughts on this wonderful ethos.

KM: I feel super strongly about this. I was 50 pounds heavier that I am now before I was 30 and it's made me the person I am today; I wouldn't change it for anything. It truly baffles me that most luxury designers won't cater for anyone over a size 12—utterly bizarre—not to mention short-sighted from a commercial perspective. I know Mary Katranzou will make her dresses in any size required—she's made a size 24 before and I totally adore her for that. Inclusivity is at the heart of converting clothes—it unleashes the gates of glorious creativity and high fashion for any shape, size and ability. It's not just about making things pretty—it liberates both garment and wearer: clothes can easily be adapted for people who struggle or have issues with their body and the way it functions which means they can't find great fashion to fit them. Suddenly they can—they can convert and be their own designer with the help of a good dressmaker (and there are many around—even in the local dry cleaner; these people are gems!).

Fashion for me is about making people feel beautiful. It has the power to gift huge confidence through feeling comfortable in the visual layer we present to the world. As our bodies change shape over time we can feel imprisoned by the size on the label and upset when clothes no longer fit us. By converting, we can take control of our clothes, making them bigger, smaller or restyling them to suit us. We never have to feel less-than if we don't fit into something—with a few simple converting tips and hacks clothes can fit again and look beyond fabulous (DM me for help! @convertedcloset). No need need to hit the gym or go on a diet—just tweak the fit with the help of a dress maker and strut that sustainable stuff!

FDL: Fashion has been transformative for your self acceptance—could you speak a little on your style journey?

KM: I started tweaking my clothes because I didn't like the way I looked in them as they were. Coming from a family of bean poles (and not being one) was hard to accept and I sought ways to achieve the optical illusion around my body I instinctively knew how to create. It's possible to draw attention to certain areas of the body and distract from others and I wanted this power. It wasn't a perfect solution but it went a long way to building up confidence and developing sense of personal style. Having the tools and freedom to be able to present my best self to the world was a huge game-changer for me.

My style is constantly evolving and smart-styling has become my saving grace. Each morning I start planning my outfit from the feet up: is it a socks or tights kind of day? I keep this drawer very exciting and slightly bonkers, design-wise, so whatever happens, my outfit will have character. Is this normal?! How do you decide what to wear Faye?

Don't you love how fashion can dramatically affect your mood? And oh boy, the things you can do with scarves, belts and jewelry right?! I salute you sister for being one of the most creative people I've ever witnessed in the realm of accessories—your creativity knows no bounds. All-Hail-Queen-Faye and her vast collection of Opshopulent brooches!

I believe *every* person on the planet harbors an inner designer. We know instinctively what style of clothes we prefer to wear and that's our inner designer talking! Some people tell me they wish they had more confidence to push their 'style-edge' further and I show them how, by converting pre-owned garments, they can explore new styles incrementally through incorporating different elements they're attracted too, in stages.

FDL: I like to call what we do future fashion. What do you predict for the future of pre-loved and conscious chic, especially post-COVID?

KM: This is future fashion Faye—well said! My prediction is that designers will continue to reign as gods of the New Fashion World but what I think they'll become more accessible to consumers. I can imagine a day where designers share techniques they use to create iconic design features so those who would like to, can convert pre-owned clothes to incorporate them. I believe sewing machine sales will continue to escalate and designer garment patterns will start becoming available. Christopher Raeburn was much revered for sharing a simple bucket hat design pattern—people loved that! Fabric accessories, or Convertibles as I call them, are such a fantastic way of using up fabric scraps, and can radically elevate any outfit! You can't buy bespoke bags, hats and hairbands to match your outfit on the High Street. But with a nifty pattern, you can create magical pieces out of fabric scraps you have left over from your conversion, adding yet more outfit value. The drive to be sustainable yet again leads to marvelous innovation.

> Upcycling is set to become the most powerful movement of our times. Never before has the fashion world been forced to adopt and embrace a trend in order to survive.

As awareness of environmental impact grows, more people will want to make easy tweaks to what they wear to freshen them up—especially as it will become trendy and admired. There will be also be more 'home-grown' designers creating small collections of one-off pieces at home, selling through social media platforms. Bespoke will get bigger in recognition of how value increases when we have things made especially for us, and hopefully we'll all prefer to wear our own (brand) names instead of other peoples!

FDL: **Post COVID?**

KM: Experts predict that re-sale is going to overtake traditional fashion sales within four years which is incredible! OpShops will elevate in status and attract a wider demographic as second-hand stigma becomes rightly obsolete.

One thing I'm highly cognizant of is that most people I speak to are not aware that the majority of second-hand donated clothes don't actually get sold. Those that are good enough will be shipped off-shore to vast (already textile flooded) markets and if not sold, to landfill in countries where waste facilities are not very advanced and more environmental damage occurs. I feel such a deep responsibility to show people how to discover the myriad of beautiful possibilities within the clothes they own and those they discover in Opshops—the climate clock is ticking.

Converting clothes is the key to unlocking the closet into Fashion Narnia. What could possibly be more exciting?

Velonika Pome'e
First Tongan Sports Illustrated model

FDL: I'm very inspired by your body confidence. Have you always been so proud and comfortable in your own skin?

DD: Growing up, I didn't have the confidence I have now. Everything came with time for me. I think that was the best thing to happen to me. I was not growing up too fast, allowing everything to serve its time and purpose.

FDL: Do you feel represented in the fashion industry? Have you always?

DD: I think we are taking the steps in the right direction. We have made some strides in the fashion and beauty industry to be more inclusive but it still does not completely reflect the world we live in. I would love to have more indigenous faces and stories be represented and normalize seeing ourselves in mainstream media.

FDL: You are such a shape-shifter. Can you speak a little about how you are disrupting the industry?

DD: I'm learning more about business and growing my brand. These spaces allow me to share what I'm passionate about and build community.

@veronicapomee @pasifikavoices @herownheroseries

FDL: What advice would you give to beautifully curvy and thick humans who are struggling to accept their size?

DD: I think we're learning how to unlearn so many years of self-sabotaging and self-hate. My advice is if there is something about yourself that you aren't happy with, you can choose to do something about it. We need to reclaim our power, or we'll always be seeking outside validation.

FDL: Do you thrift shop, swap, buy second hand, consignment, or vintage? If so, has pre-loved clothing expanded or elevated your personal style?

DD: Most of the pieces in my closet belong to my parents, are thrifted and

from local yard sales, or gifted. I love it because it's one of one and has a story to it. The stories are what keep family histories alive, develop a sense of understanding, and establish lasting family traditions.

FDL: What are three tips you use for styling your shape?

DD: I mostly find things that are comfortable and chic, and I like anything that accentuates my waist. I love shapewear as well. The biggest tip I can offer is not to be afraid to try new things.

Patrick Duffy
Swap Chain

FDL: How did your sustainability journey begin? Was it something that happened, an 'aha moment' or has it always been in your DNA?

PD: Caring for people and the planet has always been in my DNA, but I never would have called myself a sustainability expert or quote 'tree hugger.' I always had a general feeling of wanting to take care of our world. When the sustainability term came around and into what I do now it was an aha moment, what I was doing in my life, and for work, was part of a massive systemic problem which I wasn't attuned to. I thought I was doing good, making money, caring for people and the planet, but then when I actually realized what I was doing—like promoting the sales, PR events for brands and events, promoting fashion—I realized I was promoting people taking advantage of other people. So it took a moment for me to open my eyes and see—holy shit, there's a massive issue here—and that's when my 'aha' happened. I couldn't continue on that path with a conscience. You cannot *unsee* it. And once you've seen it, there's a responsibility. I couldn't be that guy.

FDL: Sustainability is such a broad term, it's not something you can define in one sentence. Could you give us a bit of a snapshot around what your incredible mission is, and the amazing platforms and opportunities that you are creating for community and the collective.

PD: What I do now is a culmination of my skill-set that I've honed from all my years in PR, marketing etc., just using those skills for good now. It started out with a clothing swap and that was what shook me in a good way. When I witnessed how it played out, I was like wow this is the most amazing thing in the world, and so then I knew I could turn it into something big.

So what I do now is an amplification of all those feelings, and all of those ideas in that one moment at the clothing swap, which was doing all different kinds of education. We show and tell things like how to fix your clothing, how to extend the life of your clothes etc. Invite experts like Orsola de castro, Carry Summers or Amanda Parks—people who are doing things to fix our industry.

Source map is where you can see the entire supply chain. When you can see it, you feel obliged to fix it. So I've taken all those things into a big plan, keep pushing, keep connecting, keep going, and a lot of it is tied back to the swaps. We're the ones who are consuming the fashion, that's mostly because we've been told we have no other options until now. You're empowering people in different expressions; swapping is something so simple that people get juiced about it, learning, seeing the impact, connecting community... it's very uplifting. I can't imagine doing anything else.

Explorers Club facilitates talks and forums. We get to ask the questions, build convos with experts—what a great job! Put it out on platforms where people can be inspired by it.

FDL: Opshopulence, redefining what luxury means in terms of fashion... so much of what I do is a beautiful luxury, it's not just clothing to me, it's clothing that supports community, charity, and diverts textile waste. It feels beautiful to elevate the clothes.

PD: For what I wear, the pendulum has swung from absolutely opulent, quirky and kooky to ultra-simplicity. The simplicity is in the items I select to wear, like right now I have a blue cashmere sweater I found at a clothing swap five years ago. I didn't wear it a lot when I first got it but then one day I was going on this around-the-world journey so I just kind of brought this little thing with me. The luxury with this sweater is having it for a long time and wearing it everywhere. It's my go-to, it feels great, the color is beautiful. I've worn it as a scarf, around my waist, I even turned it into harem pants—I put my legs through the arm holes, and it becomes pants.

FDL: Why do you think more people aren't on board yet? What do you think are the stumbling blocks?

PD: I think there are two kinds of people in this world (to quote the *Pink Flamingoes* film, 'my kind and assholes'), scarcity mindset people and abundance mindset people. Scarcity mindset people are the ones that are like holding on for dear life—I've gotta have more clothes, I might never get an opportunity for this Versace again, everything is more more more because they worry about having less less less. But it also applies to so many things. If you have an abundance mindset it naturally means you're ok with letting go if something comes your way and it doesn't work, if you missed out on the sale it's not a worry. There's a whole world of opportunities, you don't have that fashion FOMO. If your core is an abundance mindset you're naturally fine with going with the flow, having less, centered around the idea that you don't need stuff!

FDL: My whole body is resonating with what you're saying! My journey to sustainability or Opshopulence was quite a spiritual one. I realized I didn't need this; that having all these clothes was weighing me down. I realized it's actually more abundant and luxurious to have less and love those things, get all the wear out of them like you, Patrick. Makes me so happy to hear you say that!

PD: Capitalism comes from the idea of scarcity.

FDL: I call what we do, future fashion. It's a transformative tool. How can people get involved with what you do?

PD: Head to **@globalfashionexchange, @the_swapchain** or **@mrpatrickduffy** on Instagram and join our community.

Kira Simpson
The Green Hub

FDL: Tell us about yourself and your work with The Green Hub.

KS: The Green Hub is a resource for learning to live more sustainably. It started as my personal blog in 2015, where I was sharing mostly my fails at learning to live plastic free and has since grown to include contributors from around the world who share their experiences and advice.

We share brands, tips, and guides covering fashion, food, travel, and life—helping you make lifestyle choices that are kinder to people and the planet.

It's important for me to let people know that living more sustainably is not about sacrifice or giving up the things you love. You can find 'greener' alternatives to just about everything in your life from plastic-free food to sustainable hair salons. That's what The Green Hub is, a place for making these alternatives easily accessible for when you're ready to start learning and making changes.

I believe that our many small actions can collectively make a big difference. That we all have the power to vote, invest, and make positive lifestyle choices that empower us to become advocates for the planet.

FDL: Have you always been a green goddess or did you have an eco aha moment that made you switch and slow down?

KS: Not at all! The word sustainable wasn't even in my vocabulary growing up. But looking back I now see how conscious my mum was. We didn't have a lot of money; buying clothes from op shops was the norm for us. And books! I was at my local Salvos every Tuesday when a new delivery of books came in. We also never used things like paper towels or anything throwaway; it was all reusables and no packaged food. Treats and snacks were made from scratch and food was never wasted. I realize now that these habits were instilled in me from a young age and I unconsciously implemented some of them in my life early on. Thanks, Mum!

I studied biology and environmental science at uni and it opened my eyes

to some of the major issues facing our planet, but my sustainable lifestyle changes didn't really start until a few years later. Using more natural cleaning products was the first change I made, then I started composting. I learnt about the plastic pollution problem and invested in a reusable water bottle and coffee cup. Reducing my plastic use was one of the biggest changes and took a lot of years to find sustainable swaps.

The rest just developed from there with time and research. What we eat, where we shop, how we live, I realized these choices have the power to shape the kind of world we want to live in. Every small change opened the door to new opportunities to live a little more sustainably.

FDL: As you know, I believe in the power of making pre-loved pretty. I'm super passionate about shape-shifting how we see second hand... it busts perceptions, starts conversations and transforms thinking. I see this in glorious effect with The Green Hub, everything you do is so beautiful, considered and actually really calming to look at. Has this been a strategic approach for you with your work within the ethical lifestyle space?

KS: Oh thank you! That's lovely to hear. Photography is my creative outlet and I like to create beautiful content that has a bit of a calming vibe. I feel like it initially stemmed from the desire to shake off that 'frumpy hemp sack' stigma that surrounded sustainable fashion only a few years ago. I felt like I needed to shout from the rooftops, "Look! Sustainable can be beautiful!" Fortunately, that stigma has almost disappeared with the plethora of incredible brands now making sustainability sexy. But I guess the calm aesthetic just stuck and it's almost become our brand.

FDL: I think we rise as a collective with kindness. It's about progress not perfection. I aim to inspire and empower over preaching. What advice would you give to people just emerging into the slow-fashion movement?

KS: Over the years I have learned that living more sustainably is not about being perfect. It's about doing what you can with what you have available to you. It's about the mindset shift more than the individual actions we take. Because once you're aware of the issues like plastic pollution and climate change, you begin to understand the importance of collective action and system change. You don't become an activist overnight; it starts small with things like composting and reusables, and most importantly it's how your actions inspire and influence the people around you to change as well.

A lot of what we see on social media gives the impression that there's only one way to live more sustainably and we need to shrink ourselves to fit the mould. That if our sustainability efforts don't look like what we see other people doing online then we're not doing it 'right.' The thing is, there is no one single way to live more sustainably, there is no rule book you need to follow, no perfect ideal of what it should look like.

Learn the basics: reduce single-use plastic, eat less meat and dairy, manage your food waste, compost if you can, consume a bit less, use more eco-friendly cleaning and skincare products, make more conscious purchasing choices, educate yourself about the issues—and within all of that find what works for you, your family and your life. It's really that simple.

FDL: What makes you feel Opshopulent? For one I think this is an important moment to share our mutual plant obsession. My green babies give me such a feeling of luxe, new life and calm! But I'd love to know from a clothing perspective too. Fave brands, fabrics, initiatives...

KS: Plants definitely! I recently took all my houseplants outside for a hose off and realized how bare and stark the house looked and felt. Plants to me are a luxury; they've turned my home into a sanctuary and space I really love to be in. Plus, there are so many studies that have proven indoor plants help improve our concentration and productivity, reduce stress and boost our mood. Greenery and nature have a calming effect and help us feel more relaxed.

When it comes to fabric, linen is my go-to. I'm a practical person at heart and living in the hot, humid Gold Coast and working from home means I gravitate towards light, breathable, easy-to-wear clothing. Linen is low maintenance, looks great when it's a bit crumpled, and for me wearing linen feels luxurious. So linen and houseplants, that's Opshopulence!

Edwina Morgan & Aife O'loughlin

Salvos Stores

FDL: Ladies, can you give us a little insight into your respective roles with Salvos Stores?

EM & AO: We're both part of the Customer and Strategy Team with Salvos Stores, which is fitting as we both love getting to know our customers and building strategies to improve their experience while they shop and donate with us.

Edwina is the General Manager of Customer and Strategy and oversees a team of people who are responsible for making decisions which impact our customers. This can range from e-commerce, new product lines, contact centers and even IT. By connecting these multi-disciplinary functions, we can ensure we consider our customers in all our decision making.

Aife is the Customer Experience Manager for Salvos Stores, which is a role that manages our entire experience our customers have from the minute they start thinking about shopping with us, to their in-store or online experience as well as post purchase.

FDL: To you both: Has sustainability always been a thing for you, or did you have an eco-awakening like I did?

EM: I was aware of environmental issues as a kid and into my teens. I remember subscribing to Greenpeace as a teenager and getting the monthly newsletters that highlighted the environmental issues facing the world and how the fossil fuel industries were contributing to global warming. It wasn't until later in life that I understood the impact of various industries on global warming, including the fashion industry. Over the years I have built my knowledge on how the fashion industry impacts the environment, but more importantly how we can all be a part of the

Edwina Morgan

Aife O'loughlin

solution. That is why collaboration is so important across the whole ecosystem; because together we can make a significant and lasting difference to both our industry and planet.

AO: Sustainability hasn't always been a thing for me, certainly not from a clothing perspective anyway. I grew up in Ireland, and moved to Australia in my late-20s. Second hand wasn't a big thing in Ireland at that time, although it is growing now. I originally studied nursing for two years (so my family joke I am half a nurse), and then went on to study retail. When I moved to Australia the opportunity to work for Salvos Stores presented itself and I thought I might as well combine my love of retail with my desire to make a difference, and I haven't looked back. Working in the second hand retail market opened my eyes to just how much we already had, but also through research I learned so much about how unsustainable that is. It was a result of combining that knowledge with my love of what I do and making improvements and future-proofing this industry that I became passionate about sustainability.

FDL: Aife, how have you seen the customer demographic shift since op shopping has really come into the collective awareness? Who's shopping with us now, what do they want, what's their priority?

AO: In terms of the demographics of customers that are shopping second hand, it often surprises people that a large proportion of customers are making a choice to shop in this manner, rather than shopping second hand out of necessity. What we have found is there are a couple of motivations our customers have for shopping second hand which is either:

- Motivated by cost; looking for great quality brands or items at lower cost than buying new.
- Motivated by impact; whether that be on the social impact side of things or on the environmental impact side of things, and in many cases both!

While this has been true for a while, what we are seeing is a growth in the volume of people who are choosing second hand first or to supplement their wardrobe. What we do anticipate, however, is to follow the trends that are being seen out of the U.S. where shopping second hand is becoming incredibly popular.

- Second hand (resale and charity) are expected to be bigger than fast-fashion by 2029.
- Second hand shopping is being spurred on by Gen Z who don't see any stigma attached to shopping second hand (40% of Gen Z bought second hand in 2019).
- Customers plan on shifting more of their spending to second hand than any other channel in the next five years.
- Second hand is expected to double market share in the next 10 years[5].

The above stats from the Thred Up report lead us to believe that we will see continued interest and a growth in the popularity of shopping second hand within Australia over the coming years, which make this a really exciting time. With the charity retail sector in Australia being so proactive in planning for the future and watching these trends collectively, I believe we will see some really exciting things to come in this space in the years ahead, ensuring shopping second hand is something that is not only accessible to everyone but inspires even more Australian customers to shop second hand.

FDL: Edwina, COVID really saw Salvos Stores have to shift to digital and it was amazing to witness. What was that like from your strategy perspective and how did it change the brand for the better?

EM: COVID-19 has shifted so many things across our communities both in Australia and globally over the past 12 months, including the move to on-line shopping. Australia Post has reported a 73% year-over-year (YoY) growth in on-line shopping since the beginning of the pandemic. Luckily, e-commerce has always been a part of the Salvos Stores strategy, so at the start of the pandemic we were able to get our stores listing online pretty quickly. This was really important for both our team and customers as it meant we were able to continue engaging our team behind closed doors and provided us with a way to connect with our community of customers.

Over the past eight months we have listed over 100,000 items and connected with 24,000 customers, which has been an amazing result. E-commerce will continue to be important for our strategy moving forward, as it gives our customers more ways to shop with us, and for emerging customers it is a great way to experience second hand shopping in a traditional retail experience.

FDL: As you know, I believe in the power of making pre-loved things pretty; it busts perceptions and transforms thinking. Thank you for trusting me to dive into that at Salvos Stores! How do you think those perceptions are going as a collective? Are we getting it or do you still see op shopping obstacles for some sections of the community?

EM & AO: We've definitely seen some changes in customers' perception of second hand and this has by and large been assisted by the support of the online community. Alongside yourself, there has been a growth in people using social media to share and show off their second hand finds which absolutely myth-busts the idea that second hand means second best!

At Salvos Stores, we are passionate about creating retail environments that are easy to shop but still has the rummage factor. This means that avid op-shoppers still get the thrill of the hunt when they visit one of our stores, but it also ensures that if you are new to shopping second hand, it is accessible. We recently launched a new in-store concept in a store in Melbourne, and while we were getting ready to open, some local teenagers we were speaking to said the store looked "boujee". It was not a term familiar to either of us; we had to look it up. By definition it means luxurious in lifestyle yet humble in character and if we can continue to build boujee retail environments for people to shop second hand, we think we might just continue to shift perceptions!

FDL: Speaking of community, tell us about the Moving the Needle initiative, the vision for it is so incredible and you've already gained significant traction, including launching it in NYC.

EM & AO: Moving the Needle is a really important initiative, in our opinion, which seeks to bring the charity retail sector, retail brands and the customer together on a journey to divert textiles from landfill.

By working collaboratively, we believe that charity retail and retail brands can offer consumers solutions for the clothing they no longer need keeping them out of landfill, which is unfortunately where far too much of it ends up: 6000kg every 10 minutes! We've been working closely with Red Cross and Vinnies (NSW and VIC) to bring this initiative to life and to partner with some fantastic retail brands who share our passion and can share the message with their customers. To date, we've had support from Myer, Glam Corner, M.J Bale, Good Day Girl and Work Shop Studio. It's been brilliant to collaborate with these retailers to share the message of Moving the Needle and in many cases offer solutions to customers on donating.

When we launched Moving the Needle, we set up an empty shop in a Sydney shopping center for a week. The concept was simple: instead of buying from our store, you donated! It was a huge success, with the local community loving the concept and getting involved—and asking where they could buy the items! We had support from Sussan Ley MP to launch the event and received some great media coverage. Your social post on the concept went viral and soon we had interest from New York's re-fashion week to bring this concept there. So with some help, we managed to get this up and running in New York during the week alongside some great events to promote the concept, and it's fair to say it was a huge success.

Our hope is to continue to collaborate on this initiative in the future, building more partnerships with charity retail and retail brands but also looking at ways we can continue to innovate and create change in this space and make a real difference in the circular fashion economy in Australia.

FDL: What makes you feel Opshopulent?

EM: I think for me it is the ability to tell your own story and share in others. Whether it is through finding that unique item, putting together a great outfit, connecting with the in-store/on-line community, knowing that you are making a difference, being part of a movement, discovering the history of an item... all of these experiences add up to that feeling of Opshopulence.

One of my most treasured Opshopulent experiences was a few years ago. I was shopping in one of our stores when I saw the most beautiful velvet duster coat. As I was admiring the coat a lady approached me and explained that she had donated the coat and shared both her and the coat's story. She had purchased it back in the 1960s from an op shop in St Kilda when she was a young opera singer. She had owned the coat for over 40 years and worn it often during this time either when performing, going out for dinner or to events. Even though she had such fond memories she had decided to donate the coat. When I asked her why, she simply told me it was an opportunity to give someone else a chance to enjoy the coat, while giving back to the community. For me that is Opshopulence.

AO: Ooooh good question! On a personal level, it's finding designer items that I wouldn't ordinarily be in a position to splurge on! There is something special about getting dressed, wearing something a little luxe and knowing that you didn't have to live on two-minute noodles for months just to ensure you could afford it!

On a professional level it is connecting with our community, whether that be our in-store teams, our customers and donors or our online community. While we've got 350 stores (and counting!) and lots of customers to connect with, our community still feels close-knit and supportive of each other.

I have experienced the connection our store teams have with their local community and how they support each other, and to me that's seriously Opshopulent!

FDL: I like to call what we do future fashion. It's the business model we need to move towards—circularity, kindness, inclusivity, community. What do you both see for the future of op shopping?

EM & AO: For us, the future is in collaboration, as an industry, but also with the wider retail industry. The challenge around clothing consumption and clothing ending up in landfill is vast and something which can only be tackled through collaboration.

In the future, we would love to see a circular economy which has the charity retail sector as an integral partner ensuring that items which still have life left in them can continue to be used through selling on, and those that cannot, can be repurposed in meaningful ways.

CONCLUSION

Where to from Here?

Pyer Moss @pyermoss, *Your friends in New York Initiative*

'What I love most about this moment is that everybody is paying attention. It's hard to ignore what is going on right now. Our lives have been unilaterally put on break and we have to open our eyes, we have to look now. What we have to do now as creatives is think about how many systems we've been buying into and how many of them we can successfully destroy. We're stuck in this rut of we have to do things the old way. But the old way doesn't work. I just want you to think about what systems you are buying into, what you are innovating versus what are you emulating.

'Fashion's role right now is to observe and come up with solutions for problems. We control image but more importantly, we control self-esteem and I think that's where we can really find our way as an industry to really think about this new world, this post-COVID understanding of empathy… this post-George Floyd world of understanding, of empathy and seeing where we fit in to continue to build off those morals that we're collectively and consciously coming into. I don't want all of us to always be dependent on some prize or award to level the playing field, we don't need that and not one person is going to fix it, we just gotta buy out of that system.'

@shaqaeqrezai

10 CONSCIOUS CALLS
TO ACTION...

The Opshopulence Manifesto

1.

Choose an abundance mindset over a scarcity mindset. See the luxury in letting go of all clothing that is weighing you down whether that be your addiction to fast-fashion, clothes just taking up space in your closet or thinking you need more to be accepted, validated or cool. You'll be surprised how little you need when you really think about it. I promise you will feel lighter, emotionally and physically. It's magical.

Remember the ABC of Opshopulence:

A – bundance mindset
B – elieve in the underdog
C – are for the planet

See the opulence in thrift and second hand shopping, i.e. Opshopulence!

Less is the new *more*.

2.

Take stock of your stash, even if it's just going into your wardrobe and removing one item you know you're not wearing. Could you swap it, gift it or donate it? When you're ready to do more, dive in and declutter on a deeper level; it's so therapeutic. Jot down a list of what's missing from your closet. What do you truly need to suit your lifestyle and new-found Opshopulent mindset?

3.

Take a trip to your local thrift store or start by thrifting online first to test the waters. Donate what you have decluttered. Have a look around, try out some of my tips and tricks, say hi to the staff, see what goodies you can find on your list. Remember, these second hand havens do so much good for our planet.

4.

Check out some of the great resources mentioned in this book.

- Watch the *True Cost* documentary.
- See *The Minimalist* documentary.
- Enjoy the Good Morning *Vogue* Series.
- Have a look around the Fashion Revolution website and read their manifesto.
- Download the Good on You app so you can learn more about which brands are doing better for our planet. This will help you make more informed and ethical choices when shopping new.
- Explore The Green Hub and their ethical brand directory.
- Thrift from your couch **@salvostores** online, and while you're there,

hunt down your nearest bricks and mortar and get to know what the Salvos do a little more, or thrift online from wherever your nearest local online portal is in your part of the world.

- Be inspired by innovative creators and thought leaders like Pyer Moss, Slow Factory, Fashion for all and many more.
- Dive into the additional learning I have created for you... (on my site **opshopulence.com**).

5.

Come and join the community.

Jump on Instagram and follow all the fabulous eco-warriors featured in Opshopulence. They have much wisdom to impart plus they are part of my gorgeous green gang and you are so welcome to join us. It's a safe space to learn, experiment and express your Opshopulence with a like-minded tribe.

Faye De Lanty
@fayedelanty

BUY THE STORY

S-hop small, sustainably, slow
T-hrift to empower community
O-bserve, ask Qs, take action
R-euse
Y-es to people & planet

7:27 am · 24/4/21 · Twitter for iPhone

6.

Have your own #**wardrobeworkout** session. Be inspired by my existing themes and guests or create your own. Play dress-ups and get creative with what you already have. Igniting our inner child is powerful for the creative process and super healing for the soul. Try things on in your local thrift store, you don't always have to buy!

> 'Sometimes the default can lead to a whole new way of cutting or exploring. A slip lining or a collar that's hanging off, ancestral hand-me-downs… and you chance upon it and it's imbued with history, heritage, fabric, the cut. Often, we want to polish and smooth and over produce but actually I like that sleeve that's set in wrong; it's really cool.'
>
> John Galliano, in conversation with Nick Knight.

7.

Dive into some Fash-Ed. Look online or grab a copy of *Vogue*. Be inspired by the trends and then create your own Opshopulent take. This mag continues to subconsciously school me in the language of style. Explore fashion history; there are so many fascinating aspects woven into the fibers of our clothes. Particular faves of mine are the Edwardian and Victorian eras, also subcultures such as Punk and Buffalo.

8.

Get to know high fashion and couture designers. This world never fails to inspire me to create my Opshopulent looks. The way things fall, the cut, the sharp tailoring, whimsical fabrics, divine details are a constant source of education. Alexander McQueen, Chanel, Maison Margiela, Galliano and Gaultier are particular stand-outs for me. The Vogue Runway app is filled with all the shows, reviews and runways plus check out their individual social media platforms and websites.

Muse on what you could recreate with what you already have. There are also incredible documentaries you can watch on Dior, Yves Saint Laurent, Halston, Chanel/Karl Lagerfeld, and many, many more!

9.

Remember Opshopulence isn't about over the top glam 24/7. There are so many ways to implement Opshopulence into your everyday:

- a simple red lip
- a soft, thrifted cashmere sweater and sneakers
- vintage brooches on a classic blazer
- a lived-in and loved oversized men's tee with vintage Levis
- linen shorts, fresh white tank and strappy sandals

Easy, breezy, beautiful Opshopulent soul!

It's not just about the cute outfits; these clothes evoke a feeling of luxury for me because I know I voted with my dollar for a more diverse, caring and kind planet. Don't forget, an Opshopulence mindset is how you treat yourself and others too. Inclusivity, community, giving back, loving and high vibrational energy to heal and be of service.

> 'The consumer 100% has realized that the power lies within them because fashion has become way more democratized… It is happening in the street, it's on the news, it's in every choice they make, in every dollar they spend… Every time they spend a dollar with a designer or brand they're endorsing that brand and it's more pressure on these brands and corporations now more than ever to rise to the occasion and rise to the expectations of the consumers.'
>
> Hannah Stoudemire, Co-founder and CEO fashion for All Foundation
> @fashionforallfoundation

10.

Share your **#Opshopulence** with me on Instagram, I would absolutely love to see what looks you might create or what learnings you have uncovered. My community teaches me just as much as they say I teach them. Check out **opshopulence.com** for video how-to's and further learnings. And of course keep my book close by to come back to, take her thrifting with you, try some of the challenges, DIYs or ideas with friends and family. Do what feels good for you as you embark on your Opshopulent journey.

Let's redefine fashion luxury together

'We are existing now in an era of activism, in an era of revolution, in an era of global uprising and it's not just a moment. What's going on right now is not a moment. We are in the epoch of climate change, in the epoch of social uprising—so fashion plays a tremendous role in all of this. Essentially what it teaches us is that things need to change.'

Celine Semaan, Slow Factory @theslowfactory
(via Good Morning *Vogue* episode 'How the fashion industry needs to change')

OPSHOPULENCE
is the revolution our wardrobes have been waiting for

It is time to transform the way we adorn ourselves, dressing for divine service to self and those around us. Opshopulence is abundance beyond a brand or the latest 'must have' trend.

We make our own trends here

Opshopulence is a mindful style movement devoted to Mother Earth.

Will you dance with me?

ENDNOTES

1. Psychologytoday.com

2. *Vogue Australia* November 2020

3. Adam, Hajo; Galinsky, Adam D. (2012-07-01). "Enclothed cognition". *Journal of Experimental Social Psychology*. 48 (4): 918–925. doi:10.1016/j.jesp.2012.02.008. ISSN 0022-1031.)

4. 'The definition of the soul that made Oprah cry' https://www.youtube.com/watch?v=40lDcTKL4Uk

5. Thred Up Report https://www.thredup.com/resale/#future-of-fashion

BIBLIOGRAPHY

The True Cost Documentary, www.truecostmovie.com

The Minimalist documentary, www.theminimalists.com

Good on you app, www.goodonyou.eco

Ethical Clothing Australia, ethicalclothingaustralia.org.au

Fashion Revolution, www.fashionrevolution.org

Global Fashion Exchange, www.globalfashionexchange.org

The Green Hub, www.thegreenbubonline.com

Vogue Runway, www.vogue.com

Salvos Stores, www.salvosstores.com.au

Dr Anita Vandyke—Books A Zero Waste life and A Zero Waste Family, www.anitavandyke.com

Converted Closet, www.convertedcloset.com

Ellen Macarthur Foundation, www.ellenmacarthurfoundation.org

United Nations, www.undp.org

Textile beat, www.textilebeat.com

Wayne Dyer, www.drwaynedyer.com

Sojo app, www.sojo.uk

The V&A Museum, www.vam.ac.uk

Fashion for All, www.fashionforallnyc.org

The Slow Factory, slowfactory.foundation

Enclothed Cognition, en.wikipedia.org/wiki/Enclothed_cognition

www.sciencedirect.com/science/article/abs/pii/S0022103112000200

The Eco Age, www.eco-age.com

Thred Up, www.thredup.com

Moving the needle, www.movingtheneedle.com.au

The Psychology of Fashion, psychology.fashion

www.everyhuman.com.au

www.pinterest.com.au/fashionhound

www.runwayofdreams.org

www.ted.com/talks/mindy_scheier_how_adaptive_clothing_empowers_people_with_disabilities

www.vogue.co.uk

www.vogue.com.au

chopra.com/articles/the-7-spiritual-laws-of-success

Nothing New: A history of second hand by Robyn Annear, www.booktopia.com.au/nothing-new-robyn-annear/book/9781922268303.html

Mary Portas, www.weareportas.com

ekoluv.com

www.seashepherd.org.au

lessstuffmoremeaning.org/mindfullywed-eguide

www.refashionnyc.org

Loved Clothes Last Orsola de Castro, www.penguin.com.au/books/loved-clothes-last-9780241461167

Visit Opshopulence.com
for further study in the art of Opshopulence

GLOSSARY OF TERMS
A THRIFT-SAURUS

Charity shop: What the Brits call 'thrifting.' A shop where second hand goods are sold to raise money for a charity.

Circular economy: An economic system aimed at eliminating waste via the continual use of resources. It employs elements such as reusing, recycling and sharing.

Circular fashion: A circular fashion industry is one in which waste and pollution are designed out. Products and materials are kept in use for as long as possible.

Closed loop/'keep it in the loop': A system where products are designed, used and handled so as to circulate within society for as long as possible. Maximum usability, minimum adverse environmental impacts, minimum waste generation and with the most efficient use of water, energy and other resources.

Converted fashion/a converted closet: Elevating existing clothing into an exciting new form. This extends the life of the clothes and keeps our wardrobe in the loop. It also shifts perceptions of pre-loved. *Akin to Opshopulence.*

DIY: Do It Yourself is the method of building, modifying or repairing things without the direct aid of experts or professionals.

Eco-friendly: Earth-friendly or not harmful to the environment. This term most commonly refers to products that contribute to 'green living' or practices that help conserve resources like water and energy.

Ethical fashion: Is an umbrella term to describe ethical fashion design, production, retail and purchasing. It covers a range of issues such as working conditions, exploitation, fair trade, sustainable production, the environment, and animal welfare.

Fair Trade: Simply put, describes an international movement that strives to assist manufacturers and producers in developing-countries to take advantage of better trade deals. The goals of this movement include ensuring everyone gets a fair deal on pricing and better working conditions.

Plus, ethical trade encourages improvements in the communities where clothing and textiles are produced.

Fripe/la Fripe: How the French say thrift.

Greenwashing: A term used to describe situations where companies mislead consumers by claiming to be eco-friendly or sustainable as a marketing scheme rather than as a core principle of their business model. Often, these industries spend more money making themselves appear sustainable than they do implementing actual sustainable measures into their company.

Opshopulence: How to make thrift-store clothing look like couture. To elevate second hand to first-class chic. *Also see your new Mantra and abundant fashion mindset.*

Op Shop: What Australian's call 'thrifting.' It's short for Opportunity Shop. The term was actually coined by Lady Millie Tallis in the Melbourne winter of 1925.

Recycling: Converting waste material into new objects. For example, plastic bottles into jeans, an old shoe into a plant pot, wooden pallets into a table or bed.

Slow-fashion movement: Slow-fashion is about consuming and creating fashion consciously and with integrity. It connects social and environmental awareness and responsibility with the pleasure of wearing beautiful well-made and lasting clothing (as compared to the immediate gratification of fast-fashion).

Supply chain: A clothing supply chain traces all parts of the process from concept to customer, which go into creating a consumer product. This includes where and what materials are sourced, how they are developed into something larger, and the journey the finished item takes in order to arrive in store or on your doorstep.

Sustainability: The ability to be maintained at a certain level. The avoidance of the depletion of natural resources in order to maintain an ecological balance. As discussed, there is no *one way* to be sustainable. Sustainability is a deep dive, and I hope I've opened your eyes to some of its many expressions with this book.

Thrift: The quality of using money and other resources carefully and not wastefully.

Thrift flip: Making something entirely *new to you* by reinventing it. Thrift flipping borrows a term from the real estate industry. 'Flipping' refers to buying a property, doing some work on it, and selling it for more than you paid. So in the context of *thrift flipping*, it can refer to taking inventory of your closet or thrift-store finds and selling these second hand items for more than you paid for them, or reimagining your clothes with clever DIY tricks and upcycling prowess.

Thrifting: Refers to the act of shopping at a thrift store, flea market, garage sale, or the shop of a charitable organization, usually with the intent of finding interesting items at a low price.

Upcycling: Also known as 'creative reuse.' Upcycling is the process of transforming by-products, waste materials or unwanted products into new materials perceived to be of greater quality or artistic value.

Zero waste: A set of principles focused on waste prevention. It encourages the redesign of resource life cycles so that all products are reused. The goal is for no trash to be sent to landfills, incinerators, or the ocean. Currently only 9% of plastic is actually recycled.

COLLOQUIAL/FAYE-ISMS

Bad and Boujee: Hip Hop slang for something luxurious in lifestyle yet humble in character.

Basically means your outfit is fire!

Also see *Opshopulence*

Chanello: How to say hello in Chanel. (Taken from the *Sex and The City* series.) In this instance it's a term to use when something looks high-end but it was low cost and low impact on the planet.

Also see *Bad and Boujee or Opshopulence*

Glam-bulance: When something is so eco-chic you fear you may pass out. 'Please, *somebody call me a Glambulance.*'

Thrifterhood: *The thrifterhood is real...* A play on the phrase 'the sisterhood is real.' Expressing my gratitude for the kindness of the thrift community at large. It is such a vibe.

Thrifty Cent: A play on the rapper 50 Cent.

Also see *Opshopulence*.

Thrifteralla: A savvy sista who can turn rags to riches.

Couture-ify: The art of adding a couture inspired element to thrift clothing.

ACKNOWLEDGMENTS

Wow, writing a book is a beast and a half! So many angels helped me get here and I just wanted to take a moment to express my gratitude.

My dad Mick and mum Nadia for equipping me with equal parts of your Opshopulent selves and for always showing me that all my dreams are possible.

To my beautiful husband Lee, you are the most divine partner a girl could ask for. Thank you for believing in me and my thrifty vision even before I did. For never tiring of helping me take photos or modelling my Opshopulent creations. (Even though you're probably rolling your eyes on the inside!)

Salvos Stores, particularly Matt, Edwina and Aife for bestowing me with the opshop-portunity of a lifetime, a dream job that I treasure every single day, your support and faith in my fashion fairy tale has been life changing. My warrior tribe of an Instagram community... could I love you anymore!? You are a total vibe, so kind not only to me but to each other. It is an honor and pleasure to serve you and to grow with you on our eco journey. You inspire and teach me as much as you say I do for you. My best friend Karen, even though we are worlds apart these days; you, and what you did for me is forever in my heart, angel. Cherrie Bottger and the *Totally Wild* team, to begin my journey with such an incredible show, which taught me to the true art of story telling... to this day I use the wisdom this incredible 10-year adventure gifted me. Freddy and Neville for giving me my start in the charity sector, thank you for seeing me, thank you for believing in me and my slow-fashion dream.

To the amazing Vivienne Maher—photographer and creative incarnate—thank you for seeing my vision and capturing it so beautifully with the images for this book. Your work has made my words come to life in a way that still makes me weep!

The same goes for my 'fire child' Indi Field. You may not be my birth daughter but I know you are from another lifetime. I cannot begin to explain what your stunning illustrations have given to my book. They are just perfection, as are you. Thank you so much for all your hard work, darling girl. So happy the world gets to see your creative genius.

Anthea **@antheabmua** thank you for your beautiful glam on the studio images.

My gorgeous models from all over the world, thank you for taking the time to create such beauty from your very own wardrobe, its just so wonderful to have you featured.

Julie, my book angel. I wouldn't be here without you and your team. So much love for Sophie and Amanda too.

My friends Sam and Marcia for introducing me to Julie. This meeting, is where the Opshopulence journey could finally take flight.

Blessings and extreme gratitude to you all,
beautiful souls.

AUTHOR CONTACT

If you would like to see more of Faye's work be sure to connect and engage via her social media portals.

To work with Faye, please send requests by email.

Email	faye@fashionhound.tv	Instagram	@fayedelanty
Website	www.fashionhound.tv	Twitter	@fayedelanty
Facebook	FashionHoundOfficial	Linkedin	Faye De Lanty
YouTube	Faye De Lanty		

Did you enjoy reading this book?

If so, it would be wonderful if you could please take a few moments to post a positive review on Amazon.

Share your thoughts on what you loved about the book so
that others can benefit from your experience of Opshopulence.

In turn, they can enjoy it too.
Thank you so much!

Love,
Faye De Lanty.

www.ingramcontent.com/pod-product-compliance
Lightning Source LLC
Chambersburg PA
CBHW062031290426
44109CB00026B/2592